MODERN WORLD NATIONS

AFGHANISTAN	IRAQ
ARGENTINA	IRELAND
AUSTRALIA	ISRAEL
AUSTRIA	ITALY
BAHRAIN	JAMAICA
BERMUDA	JAPAN
BOLIVIA	KAZAKHSTAN
BOSNIA AND HERZEGOVINA	KENYA
BRAZIL	KUWAIT
CANADA	MEXICO
CHILE	THE NETHERLANDS
CHINA	NEW ZEALAND
COSTA RICA	NIGERIA
CROATIA	NORTH KOREA
CUBA	NORWAY
EGYPT	PAKISTAN
ENGLAND	PERU
ETHIOPIA	RUSSIA
FRANCE	SAUDI ARABIA
REPUBLIC OF GEORGIA	SCOTLAND
GERMANY	SOUTH AFRICA
GHANA	SOUTH KOREA
GUATEMALA	TAIWAN
ICELAND	TURKEY
INDIA	UKRAINE
IRAN	UZBEKISTAN

MODERN WORLD NATIONS

Uzbekistan

Thomas R. McCray
Columbia College, Missouri

Series Consulting Editor
Charles F. Gritzner
South Dakota State University

CHELSEA HOUSE
PUBLISHERS
A Haights Cross Communications Company

Philadelphia

Frontispiece: Flag of Uzbekistan

Cover: Rail transport is important to the economy of Uzbekistan.

CHELSEA HOUSE PUBLISHERS

VP, NEW PRODUCT DEVELOPMENT Sally Cheney
DIRECTOR OF PRODUCTION Kim Shinners
CREATIVE MANAGER Takeshi Takahashi
MANUFACTURING MANAGER Diann Grasse

Staff for UZBEKISTAN

EXECUTIVE EDITOR Lee Marcott
PRODUCTION EDITOR Megan Emery
ASSOCIATE PHOTO EDITOR Noelle Nardone
SERIES DESIGNER Takeshi Takahashi
COVER DESIGNERS Keith Trego
LAYOUT 21st Century Publishing and Communications, Inc.

Library of Congress Cataloging-in-Publication Data

McCray, Thomas R.
  Uzbekistan / by Thomas R. McCray.
      v. cm. — (Modern world nations)
  Includes index.
  Contents: Uzbekistan a pivotal state — Physical environment — Uzbekistan across time
— People and their culture — Government — Uzbekistan's economy — Regional contrasts
— Uzbekistan looks ahead.
  ISBN 0-7910-7915-5
  1. Uzbekistan—Juvenile literature. [1. Uzbekistan.] I. Title. II. Series.
DK948.66.M38 2004
958.7—dc22

                                                                    2003027780

Table of Contents

1 Uzbekistan: A Pivotal State   8

2 Physical Environment   12

3 Uzbekistan Across Time   26

4 People and Their Culture   32

5 Government   44

6 Uzbekistan's Economy   54

7 Regional Contrasts   74

8 Uzbekistan Looks Ahead   92

   Facts at a Glance   96
   History at a Glance   100
   Further Reading   102
   Index   104

Uzbekistan

1

Uzbekistan: A Pivotal State

O n Christmas Day of 1991, the Union of Soviet Socialist Republics (USSR), an area covering all of northern Asia and half of Europe and a principal adversary of the United States and its allies, broke apart and collapsed. The long and bitter cold war, a defining struggle in world affairs for a half-century, simply ended. Now, years later, the United States and its allies are again spending tremendous military, economic, and political resources in an attempt to achieve peace—this time in southern and southwestern Asia. U.S. involvement in Iraq and Afghanistan, with Palestine and Israel, with Turkey and Iran, and with Pakistan and India has achieved a level that some now call a "new defining struggle in world affairs." In a pocket of territory located between these two great centers of strategic importance lies a country that stands apart from both of them. That country is Uzbekistan.

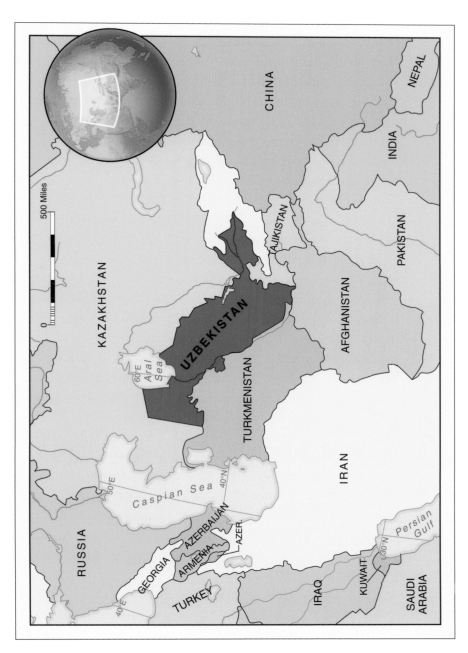

Uzbekistan is about the size of California and is located deep within the Eurasian landmass. It is one of the five nations in Central Asia that were part of the Soviet Union before they received their independence in 1991.

Uzbekistan has an area of about 173,000 square miles (448,000 square kilometers). It is about the size of California (but with several million fewer people) and is located deep within the world's largest landmass—Eurasia. Like its neighbors, Turkmenistan to the south, Kazakhstan to the west and north, and Kyrgyzstan, Tajikistan, and Afghanistan to the east, the country's name carries the suffix -*istan*, which means "land of." Physical landscapes vary from high mountains in the southeast to parched deserts in the central and western parts of the country. In the west, fertile oases of the Amu Darya and Syr Darya give way to the rapidly shrinking Aral Sea—one of the world's worst environmental disasters.

Uzbekistan has enough farmland, oil, gold, and water to build a prosperous economy, but it is generally poor by Western standards. It is a country surrounded by clouds of warlordism, Islamism, capitalism, authoritarianism, colonialism, and halting democracy. It is a country with a classic strongman leadership, stubbornly corrupt institutions, and serious environmental handicaps. Despite their country's many problems, Uzbekistanis are a remarkably patient, self-reliant, and optimistic people; they take pride in a heritage reaching back as far as civilization itself. Culturally, Uzbekistan has a powerful and long-standing regional influence; it is a leading middle Asian nation.

Regional and global demand for Uzbek resources is strong and growing. At the same time, however, much of the country's economic fate lies beyond its control, guided by circumstances and policies of other countries. Neighboring countries often make front-page news in the United States and Europe, but Uzbekistan remains little known and underappreciated in the Western world. This is true even though the country is friendly to the United States and Europe and has become a frontline player in the global war against terrorism.

Uzbekistan is a land of natural wonders and awesome beauty, but it is also a place of infamous environmental catas-trophe. It has a history of unresponsive government; its people are accustomed to dictatorial rule, bad government planning, and economic hardship. Uzbekistanis are not dismayed by slow progress. Most of what they want and expect from their leaders is a degree of stability in their lives and daily activities.

Until the late twentieth century, Uzbekistan was practically sealed off from the rest of the world. Today, it still is remote and is still a long way from having an open society. It is, at the same time, a place where outsiders can truly get away from the "daily grind" of frantic commercialism or concerns about success and failure measured against the proverbial bottom line. Life in Uzbekistan walks at a slower pace and, in many respects, feels almost detached from the global issues that swirl about the world beyond.

Uzbekistan is an important place for Americans to study and understand. Of key importance to Westerners is the fact that Uzbekistan offers us an opportunity to "get it right." It challenges us to develop positive relations with a Muslim country, to cultivate the right outlook for a country formerly a part of the Soviet Union, to convey a positive message to and cultivate a strategic position in an otherwise deeply troubled part of the world.

Through the pages of this book, you will visit this little-known country. You will travel through its varied natural landscapes and wander the corridors of its long and fascinating history. You will visit its people in their daily lives and communities. Your tour will take you through the inner workings of the country's government and its economic activities. Finally, you will take a glimpse into the country's future potential.

2

Physical Environment

U zbekistan (Land of Uzbeks) is a landlocked country that stretches from high mountain ranges in the southeast to the parched Turin Basin in the northwest, with wide grassy steppes in between. At its southeastern end, high mountain systems reach like fingers extending deep into the interior lowlands from the hand of Central Asia's *Pamir Knot*, or "Roof of the World." Here, they capture rainfall for various segments of rich, grassy steppelands; they also cradle the fertile Fergana Valley. The mountainous edges of Uzbekistan and of the greater basin region are constantly folding at the margins, because of the collision of surrounding subcontinental plates. The edges of this greater area form a belt of violent tectonic activity. In neighboring Turkmenistan, the capital city of Ashgabat was leveled by an earthquake in 1947, as was Uzbekistan's capital city, Tashkent, in 1966 and 1967.

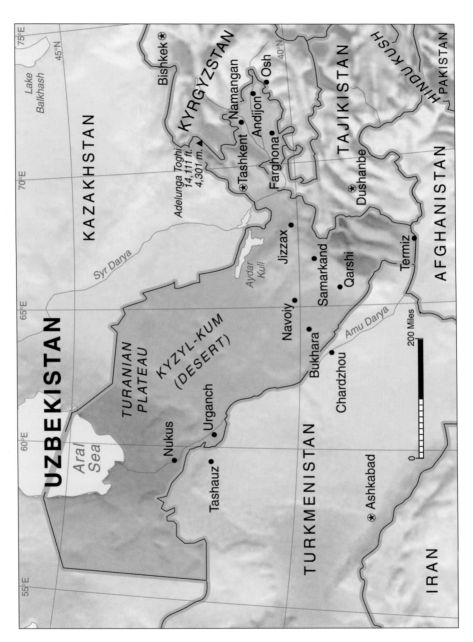

Uzbekistan's physical landscapes range from very high mountains in the southeast to parched deserts in the central and western parts of the country. The fertile oases of the Amu Darya and Syr Darya give way to the Aral Sea in the far west.

Much of Uzbekistan's steppelands and its entire western basin rest on an ancient saline seabed layer. As the ancient Tethis Sea grew shallower and ultimately evacuated the Turin Basin 200 million years ago, seawater sediments became concentrated here. Today, billions of tons of salt lie beneath 70 percent of the Turin Basin, extending to a depth of about ten feet (three meters). The presence of this salt layer is important for two reasons. First, naturally saline soils lock up a portion of available water, thereby denying it to plants. They are an impediment to farming, Uzbekistan's main economic activity. Second, this layer of salt has sealed-in natural gas and oil in such huge quantities that the basin is believed to hold one of the top three or four hydrocarbon reserves in the world. Uzbekistan is at the core of this basin.

WATER: THE CONTROLLING RESOURCE

The climate of Uzbekistan is mostly midlatitude desert. Conditions can be as hot and dry as those in Arabia or the Sonora Desert of Northern Mexico but with much colder winters. Precipitation ranges from 4 to 12 inches annually (8 to 30 millimeters) and potential evaporation averages 68 inches (1,700 millimeters), a combination of conditions that create a dry and often barren landscape. On average, the sky remains cloudless 180 days, approximately half the year. This extreme dryness is explained by the region's location in the interior of the vast Eurasian landmass— far removed from ocean-driven weather. Uzbekistan is roughly the same distance north of the equator as southern Europe or the central United States, and Uzbekistan's weather similarly comes from the west. Unfortunately, for the Uzbeks, spring rains are much weaker than they are in Spain or California because Uzbekistan's segment of the westerly winds does not bring moist air masses directly from a great ocean. After crossing the Mediterranean Sea, most moisture is wrung from advancing air masses over Turkey and other lands west of the Caspian Sea, leaving little to fall on Uzbekistan.

In winter, extremely cold air invades from the north, driving bone-chilling, arctic-continental surface winds against the surrounding ranges of the Tien Shan Mountains in the east and the Pamirs and Alay mountains in the south. These northwest-facing barriers intercept winter and spring moisture; the air masses are formed over land and therefore are rather dry. Their cold temperatures make them so heavy that they push away any wetter and lighter air masses. Winter therefore does not bring much precipitation to Uzbekistan.

Historically, evaporation from the Aral Sea has returned as rain or snow, falling on Uzbekistan's eastern mountains. This moisture has accounted for a sizeable portion of the region's total runoff. Additional atmospheric moisture is provided by the steady evaporation of soil moisture pulled up from groundwater reserves under the plains and by transpiration from the grasses of the sprawling steppes. Most rain that falls within this region is lost rapidly to evaporation. Of the rain that falls on the greater Turin Basin every year, more than 85 percent is lost almost immediately to evaporation and deep percolation. Over the rugged mountains of the region's perimeter, an average year brings about 22 inches (550 millimeters) of precipitation; 7.6 inches (191 millimeters) of this precipitation resists evaporation back into the atmosphere and begins to flow downslope.

Uzbekistan's dryness can be attributed to its position at the core of a great landmass. Tropical moist air from the Arabian Sea is blocked from reaching the Asian interior by towering mountains. Distant from the ocean, situated in the world's largest and coldest inhabited landmass, and surrounded by high mountain barriers, Uzbekistan is in a rain shadow.

Obviously, the controlling resource in a desert is water, and none of Uzbekistan receives abundant rainfall. In contrast, its eastern neighbors, the mountainous republics of Kyrgyzstan and Tajikistan, receive considerable amounts of precipitation. As the semiarid air masses blow eastward across Uzbekistan, they release hardly a drop of moisture.

When they are forced to climb over the high Tien Shan and Pamir ranges, however, they eventually drop much of their remaining moisture on the mountains' west-facing slopes. This means that 9 percent of Uzbekistan's water supplies originate on home territory and 91 percent originates in the neighboring republics and flows into the country from these eastern highlands.

Fresh water deliveries into Uzbekistan result from spring rainfall, late spring snowmelt, and late summer melt waters from high mountain glaciers. This glacial melt brings a second high-water mark when it is most needed for late season irrigation. In the case of the Amu Darya, glacial thaw contributes about 14 percent of the total high mountain runoff but 44 percent of runoff in the rainless summer months. These high mountain glaciers also moderate the differences between wet and dry years. Years of low rainfall usually coincide with increased glacial thawing, and years of high rainfall coincide with increased glacial storage.

Since the low Aral Sea Basin spreads over the western parts of Uzbekistan, runoff from precipitation on the eastern mountains drains westward toward that basin. From the mountainous zones of Central Asia, 88 percent of runoff is carried on the surface; the rest migrates as groundwater. A bit lower—on the Uzbek steppes—60 percent of precipitation flows on the surface and 40 percent migrates as groundwater. The "exotic" surface waters (so named because they originate in a more humid distant area) are dammed, stored, and diverted into irrigation networks for Uzbekistan's fields and farms. Everywhere in Uzbekistan, evaporation causes a significant loss of surface water. Regarding groundwater, the water tables continue to drop as they descend into the lowland deserts of the Turin Basin. Knowing how near the groundwater levels are to the surface is very important in an area where irrigation water is being applied from the top down.

Nowhere in the country receives abundant rainfall due to its location at the core of a great landmass. Mountains such as the Pamir Range shown, draw out water from the semiarid air masses and feed river water supplies.

ENVIRONMENTAL TRAGEDY OF THE ARAL SEA

Located at the bottom of the Turin Basin, the Aral Sea has no outlet except evaporation. It was, until the 1960s, the world's fourth-largest landlocked water body (in surface area), after the Caspian Sea and lakes Superior and Victoria. Aral has always been shallow for its great size, but 40 years ago, the sea began to shrink. By the early twenty-first century, its water

These boats are abandoned at the edge of the shrinking Aral Sea. Many fishermen kept the local fishing industry alive until there was no water to keep their fishing boats afloat.

level had dropped 50 feet (about 15 meters), its surface had lost 60 percent of its area, and its volume had shrunk by 75 percent. The disappearance of the Aral Sea was a process set in motion 70 years ago, when large amounts of water were increasingly diverted from its two main tributaries—the Amu Darya and Syr Darya (*darya* means "river" in Turkish languages). These two rivers, carrying freshwater from the southeastern mountains into and through Uzbekistan and flanking it on the north and south, are also middle Asia's two most voluminous streams. The Syr is formed by the meeting of Kyrgyzstan's Kara Darya and Naryn River at the high eastern end of the Fergana Valley, a rich agricultural area. The Amu is formed by the confluence of the Vakhsh and the Pyandzh rivers of Tajikistan, which drain the Pamir Mountains and other highland glacier fields in the region. Historically and naturally, the Syr poured life-giving water into the northern Aral, and the Amu delivered twice as much into the southern part of the sea. Together, these two rivers provided 87 percent of the Aral inflow, with the rest coming from precipitation and groundwater seepage.

With so much summer heat, large areas of good soil, large exotic streams, and so many cloudless days, Uzbekistan is an agricultural treasure. Its grassy steppes are some of the most productive farmland in all of middle Asia—an area stretching from the Caspian Sea to western China and from central Afghanistan north to the broad plains of Kazakhstan. This might seem surprising to those who think of arid lands as being hostile to life. They are, after all, relatively barren landscapes. Plants, however, thrive on mineral-rich soils, and desert soils—even when dry and heavily mineralized— are typically fertile. Their minerals have never been leached down and away from the root zone by frequent rains. For as long as Uzbekistan was colonized by the Russian and Soviet empires, it was forced to grow an important crop that Russia could not produce in sufficient quantities anywhere else in its vast and cold territory: cotton. Uzbekistan has long yielded a wide variety of fine fruits and melons, vegetables, nuts, and grains. Silk was produced there 1,500 years ago. Under Russian rule, however, Uzbekistan was ordered to grow cotton. This policy of "cottonization" radically rearranged Uzbekistan's landscape, overworked its desert soils and over-drew available water supplies, and did so in the name of the Soviet economy.

An Altered Physical Environment

For thousands of years, the steppes, valleys, oases of the Aral Sea Basin have supported hydraulic societies—societies based on and ordered by access to water. Bukhara's Abdulla Khan developed an elaborate water infrastructure in the last quarter of the sixteenth century, and the main canal still has landings where children and clothes were washed at that time. In Samarkand, the Dargom canal system has been running continuously for 2,000 years. The Great Fergana Canal, dug in the 1930s, is thought to have traced a much older route. Despite the persistence of ancient waterworks, people of the region conformed to the limits of natural environmental systems. River channels and community wells historically defined the extent of local authority over water.

Then came the nineteenth and twentieth centuries and a series of political and economic decisions imposed from outside the region. The lands of today's Uzbekistan were turned into a center for growing cotton, one of the world's thirstiest crops. This program of cottonization would require the literal replumbing of the Turin Basin. For almost 100 years, cottonization diverted increasing amounts of water from natural streams and into huge man-made irrigation systems that included reservoirs and an extensive network of canals. As a result of this strategy, the agricultural productivity of Uzbekistan and the very existence of important natural systems are now both severely threatened. The threat has come through increased demands on finite resources—specifically, good farmland and fresh water. All of this diverted water, under natural conditions, was destined for the Aral Sea.

The Aral Catastrophe

The Aral Sea once supported a prosperous fishing industry, employing tens of thousands of workers in fishing and factory ships at sea and in the canneries on shore. Its shallow-water reed beds provided fiber for paper and cover for healthy populations of birds and mammals. On the Aral's southern and eastern shores, the Kara Kalpak people maintained a seminomadic lifestyle based on trapping, hunting, farming, and trading. Along their winding paths to the sea, the Syr Darya and Amu Darya fed numerous smaller lakes and wetlands, and where these rivers met the sea, rich and sprawling deltas supported animal husbandry and many kinds of crops. The Amu, plowing as it does through the sandy Kara Kum (Red Desert), carries more silt by volume than nearly any other river in the world. For this reason, the Amu Delta is especially large and historically productive. This was the natural water arrangement and traditional economy of the Aral Sea until very recently.

The effects of water diversions on the Aral Sea were gradual and not apparent for several decades. At first, marshlands along the courses of the two great rivers began to dry up, and this was commonly attributed to climatic fluctuation and even to geologic activity such as earthquakes. Then the natural chain lakes on the lower river courses started to disappear. Finally, the problem of water diversions hit the Aral Sea directly, and the damaging effects have steadily advanced. Today, the reed beds that once flourished along the Aral's eastern shore are gone, as are the mammals that thrived near its waters and the migratory birds that flocked to its surface. Gone, too, are all the commercial fisheries and related jobs. After a long incubation period, what many see as the sudden demise of the Aral Sea has come to pass. This did not happen suddenly or as a result of naturally occurring conditions. It is the result of human arrogance and the mismanagement of a fragile natural environment, a situation that many scientists regard as the world's greatest identifiable ecological catastrophe.

Starving the Aral Sea of freshwater inflow has revealed a thick crusty seabed that is coated with natural sea salts, soil salts accumulated from irrigation runoff from millions of acres of cotton fields, and toxins that have been drained carelessly from agricultural fields into the rivers and washed downstream for

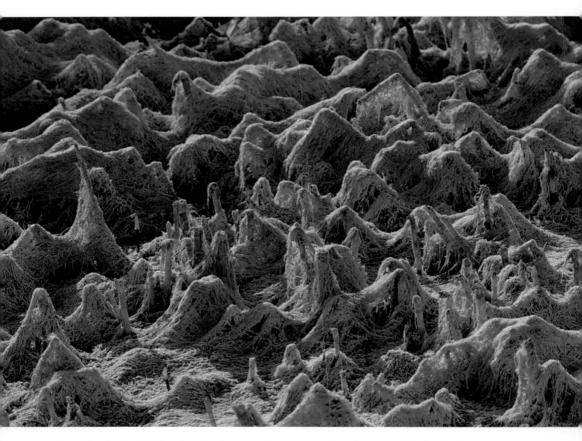

The lack of inflowing fresh water has created stark scenes in the Aral Sea where the thick crusty seabed has been exposed. The sea is a giant saltwater lake that was once the fourth-largest inland body of water in the world, but it is shrinking due to overuse and evaporation.

decades. This spreading wasteland, which now covers 15,600 square miles (40,000 square kilometers), is locally referred to as *Aral Kum* (Aral Desert). Backtracking upstream from the Aral, observers can see that as the volume of fresh river water has declined in the Aral's two great tributaries, their concentrations of pollution have grown. What remains for farmers and citizens near the end of the line is a dirty mess of undrinkable "water" that is toxic and makes them sick. Their groundwater wells, too, have dropped to a greater depth as the level of the Aral Sea has plummeted, and that water has become dirty and contaminated from the same toxins.

The shrinking Aral Sea—or rather, the growing Aral Kum—is having a noticeable affect on the region's climate. Without the large water body, area summers are now hotter and winters are colder. The growing season is shorter, and many farmers in the region have switched from cotton to rice, which matures more quickly. Unfortunately, rice is one of the few crops that require even more water than cotton. Every year, the hot Turin Basin generates its own cyclonic dust storms. This is not new. What is new is the content of these storms. The "dust" that is lifted from this basin floor is now laced with poisonous crop additives such as the dreaded defoliant Butofos. This chemical was used to make cotton plants drop their leaves for cleaner picking, but it sickened and even killed cotton pickers for years before use in the fields was finally discontinued. It was then left to continue seeping from rusty storage barrels into the groundwater. There are poisonous pesticides, such as DDT, in the dust and unhealthy concentrations of fertilizers and natural soil minerals from field runoff. There are also petroleum contaminants, hazardous industrial wastes, and even residues from nuclear waste and municipal sludge (only half of Uzbekistan's cities and few of its villages have sewers). These particulates rain down on farmlands and people all around the Aral Basin. Among the disastrous results is a very high incidence of respiratory illnesses, an explosion in the number of throat cancers, and mothers' milk that is considered unhealthy for babies to drink.

Poisonous Aral Kum dust clouds are also spreading far beyond the local region. Salts are collecting on the faces of Asian glaciers and accelerating their melt. This could ultimately shrink Uzbekistan's rich glacial reservoirs and reduce that fortunate second high water mark discussed previously. Beyond central Asia, tons of contaminated Aral Kum dust is falling over

Pakistan, and deposits have been found inside the Arctic Basin. Contaminated salt and dust storms from the Aral seabed have even raised the level of particulate matter in Earth's atmosphere by some 5 percent; they pose a serious threat to possible global climate change.

The dying Aral Sea is at the end of a long and complex chain of water manipulations and is only the most glaring example of environmental crises in Uzbekistan that can be tied to agricultural malpractice. Cotton is notorious for depleting soils. It needs strong applications of fertilizer, particularly in the chronic absence of crop rotation—the planting of other soil-building crops in odd years. In Uzbekistan, cotton growers are also notorious for using high concentrations of toxic crop additives and especially for consuming great amounts of water. Excessive chemical applications have obvious environmental and health costs, but the danger of irrigation may not be self-evident. This is how it works.

As irrigation water is poured onto salinized soils, soil salts are dissolved when the water percolates downward. Then, as the hot desert air causes surface water to evaporate, moisture just below the surface is pulled upward, bringing dissolved salts with it. Only pure water evaporates, so the salts are left high in the soil-root zone, a condition called "secondary salinization." In Uzbekistan, 60 percent of all irrigated land is seriously salinized. In some heavily irrigated areas, the problem is even worse. In parts of the Fergana Valley, for instance, more than 80 percent of farmland is damaged in this way. In the Karakalpak Republic (the tailwater zone of the Amu Darya), almost all farmland is afflicted with harmful concentrations of surface salts.

Uzbekistan's economy is agrarian, and its serious environmental problems result from agricultural malpractice. Agricultural reform, therefore, will be essential for Uzbekistan's future economic prosperity. The consequences of overirrigating are now so great that they present an immense problem for which little time remains to respond. How the government responds will determine the health of the country's agriculture and the success of its economy. It will also reflect the integrity of Uzbekistan's politics and will chart the way for the new historical geography of a now independent Uzbekistan. Agriculture is the key to the country's economy, and its reform offers the key to the future. Both of these subjects will be investigated later in this book, but a true understanding of Uzbekistan must begin with an understanding of its past.

3

Uzbekistan
Across Time

U zbekistan lies astride one of history's greatest intersections. Alexander the Great invaded the area in 330 B.C. and found Mesopotamians (from modern-day Iraq) and other Indo-Europeans already settled around Samarkand (or Samarqand). In A.D. 710, when Muslims were spreading the teachings of Mohammed outward in every direction from what we now call the Middle East, Islam came to the city of Bukhara (or Bukhoro). When European Crusaders fought with Muslims over control of the Holy Land in the eleventh, twelfth, and thirteenth centuries, many important Islamic texts were brought to Bukhara for safekeeping, and the city became a great scholarly capital in the Islamic realm. World-class achievements in medicine, literature, and astronomy came from the steppes of today's Uzbekistan.

Uzbekistan is at the heart of Turkistan, a land conquered by Turkic Mongols and which included a huge area of central Asia. From out of modern-day Uzbekistan, the Seljuk Turks conquered Persia in 1051 and Baghdad in 1055. They also transplanted the first Turkish blood onto the Anatolian Peninsula, where today's Republic of Turkey is found. In A.D. 1170, from a base in what is today Uzbekistan, the Mongol Khan Chingis (known in the West as Genghis Khan), spread his empire over most of early Russia. Ultimately, his oppression unified the eastern Slavs as none of their own leaders had done. The Mongol hordes established the first strategic and territorial links between central Asia and Russia; they eventually pushed westward to the very edges of Western Europe. Theirs was the greatest land empire the world has ever seen.

In 1400, Timur (also known as Tamerlane) raged from Samarkand across the land of Afghanistan and conquered the Indo-Gangetic Plain and its ancient capital, Delhi. Many other early tribes passed over the hills and grasslands of modern Uzbekistan, and their ethnic signatures are written on the faces of Uzbekistanis. Alexander the Great, Genghis Khan, and Timur, however, are among the most feared and respected conquerors that humanity has ever produced, and it is in part because of these three that Uzbeks claim a well-deserved sense of grandeur and a pride of place in the heart of Asia. Their magnificent temples, cultural and linguistic imprints, golden eras of discovery and development, and their storied and savage conquests throughout much of Eurasia all left an indelible impression on the land and its people.

The Great Silk Road linking the Mediterranean seacoast with China was the first connection between Western and Eastern civilizations. This famous route ran through the lands of present-day Uzbekistan. In 1497, Vasco de Gama sailed his ships around Africa, and Europeans began to appear on Asia's southern seas. The appeal of a land route linking East and West began to fade behind the economies of scale, speed, and security of water transportation. Russia broke open the Volga River in 1556 and threw off the "Mongol Yoke" of 240 years under Genghis' Kahn's old clan. Central Asian cultures—at the hub of world civilization while Europe struggled through the Dark and Middle Ages—retreated and subdivided into a patchwork

The Ark Fortress was used by the emir of Bukhara until 1924, when the city ceased to be autonomous. Today, it is a popular tourist attraction in this historic and beautiful city.

of compressed kingdoms that languished in the shadow of modern transoceanic empires. Events that were modernizing the West—the Protestant Reformation, the Age of Discovery, the Industrial Revolution, and the rise of democracy—all avoided central Asia. Regional kings, especially the emir of Bukhara (downslope from Samarkand) and the khans of Khiva (south of the Aral Sea) and Kokand (in the Fergana Valley), fell to infighting. In this weakened state, they all became vulnerable to invasions.

ENTER THE RUSSIANS

Russia finally conquered the kingdoms of Uzbekistan, but the conquest did not happen quickly or easily. In 1717, Russia's Tsar Peter the Great sent an expeditionary force to Khiva; almost everyone was killed. In the winter of 1839–1840, another Russin march on Khiva failed, with great loss of life. Khiva, the Russians believed, would be their road to India, a route that could help them weaken British domination of that rich subcontinent. For the better part of a century, Russia and Great Britain vied for control of India's northern frontier; this rivalry came to be called the "Great Game." In the process, the gap between the two rising empires closed from 2,000 miles to mere dozens, and Middle Asia regained some of the strategic importance it had lost with the decline of the Silk Road.

In 1865, the Russians conquered Tashkent and made it their regional power base. The installation of railroads began immediately, bringing the Russian culture and army and sending shipments of cotton to Moscow. At first, the Uzbeks and others exported spun cotton, but Russia's industrial revolution, like that of Great Britain, required only raw cotton. That was sent, instead of spun cotton, in increasing amounts.

Samarkand, Khiva, and Kokand fell to Russian control in 1868, 1873, and in 1878. Finally, in 1881, the Turin Basin's last Turkic-Mongol resistance was destroyed at Goek Tepe, slightly south of today's Uzbekistan. Tsar Alexander II promptly organized the greater basin into one Russian Turkistan. He intended to subdue Russia's old enemy, the Muslim Mongols; prevent any British advances into Russia's growing regional sphere of influence; and develop and control a valuable trade in cotton. It is noteworthy that this last goal was sharpened by the Civil War in the United States (1861–1865). Russians had grown dependent on cotton exports from the southern states, and the collapse of that trading partner forced Russia to look elsewhere for this valuable fiber.

With the February 1917 Bolshevik Revolution, the Russian Empire fell. Although the Bolsheviks did not begin to take control for another eight months, the political status of the Uzbeks was suddenly thrown into doubt. In a plea for support, the Bolshevik father of the USSR himself, Vladimir Ilyich Lenin, sent greetings and a promise of self-determination to minorities throughout the old empire and specifically to the Muslims of central Asia. For the Uzbeks, there appeared to be an opportunity for greater independence. In November of that year, they seized that opportunity when the people of Kokand founded their own provisional autonomous state. It would be mostly Uzbek, but one-third of the congressional seats were reserved for non-Muslims. Although the provisional autonomous state did not speak for Bukhara or Khiva, their fates depended on how successful the new government in Kokand would be in breaking away from Russian control. That success lasted just 90 days. Lenin's promise, given the political chaos of the time, was weak, and ultimately it was broken completely. In February 1918, the Soviet response to Kokand came in a brutal assault, during which most of the city's 50,000 residents were killed. Popular resistance was met with increased force. A Muslim rebel movement fought on for almost ten more years, but despite this resistance, Uzbekistan became a republic within the Soviet Union. Obviously, the massacre at Kokand gave a menacing tone to north–south relations that lasted throughout the life of the USSR. That tone lives on even now that the Soviet Union is gone.

In most of the old Russian Empire, resistance against Bolshevism had dissipated by the early 1920s, and the Union of Soviet Socialist Republics (USSR) was born in 1922. In Uzbekistan, resistance to Soviet repression lasted considerably longer, but Lenin's Moscow government could not wait for the end of hostilities before reorganizing Turkistan. Boundaries were imposed over the region, and in 1924, the Uzbek Soviet Socialist Republic was assembled from the Khanate of Khiva and portions of the Fergana Valley that had constituted the Khanate of Kokand. The Emirate of Bukhara held on to some autonomy for a bit longer before it was also swallowed up into Uzbekistan.

Throughout the Soviet era, Uzbekis kept just as busy as they had to be, and they ignored the dictates of Moscow as much as they could. Meanwhile, the land and water resources were overworked for the benefit of the USSR. To the outside world, Uzbekistan was an uneventful place, save for an occasional earthquake or political purge. Removal by forceful overthrow or death seemed to be the favorite way to change political leadership in the country, yet over the life of the Uzbek SSR, there were only three major leadership changes. Elections were held, but they were not really contested. Moscow did not meddle in day-to-day affairs as long as the cotton came in and the people stayed quiet. With the break-up of the USSR, Uzbekistan achieved its dream of independence, declaring itself a republic on September 1, 1991. As for the Great Game players, the twentieth century mocked them both: The British lost India in 1947, and the Russians lost their grip on central Asia in 1991.

4

People and Their Culture

POPULATION

The Republic of Uzbekistan is home to 26 million people. That might not seem crowded for a country the size of California, which has 32 million people, but that part of Uzbekistan that is forested, fishable, well watered, and farmable is much smaller than comparable areas of California. In addition, California's economy is more than 20 times greater than that of Uzbekistan. Moreover, Uzbekistan's population is growing at a high rate of 1.7 percent, and 60 percent of its population is under 25, ensuring that this rate will stay high. The country's fertility rate (number of children per woman) has dropped in recent decades and is now about 3.5. Even assuming a continued drop in the growth rate (births per 1,000 people minus deaths per 1,000 people), Uzbekistan's population in 2025 should exceed 34 million.

Considering that the government's ability to protect quality land or to deliver clean water for drinking and irrigation has already been met or exceeded, it becomes clear that Uzbekistan is overpopulated. A growing population demands more public housing, more schools, and more transportation systems. It also needs more jobs, more electricity, and more health care and other public services. When these factors are considered, it becomes clear that a 36 percent population growth over the next 20 years presents a crisis situation for Uzbekistan's providers and consumers alike.

During the Soviet era, and thanks to Soviet development, the average lifespan of Uzbekistan's citizens expanded from 40 to 70 years. Soviet development, however, did not include diversifying Uzbekistan's economy, and this was a fateful error. Most of the population was kept in a farm-labor economy. Rural living encourages big families because young people can work on farms. Manufacturing, on the other hand, encourages urbanization and smaller families. Uzbekistan's population explosion began to alarm Soviet planners more than a decade before the fall of the USSR. When the breakup came in 1991, Russia's decision not to reformulate a political union with its old partner republics to the south reflected a widespread fear of being overwhelmed by central Asians. By staying separate, Russians reduced their future exposure to easy Uzbek migrations northward. In the process, however, Russia also abandoned two and a half million non-Central Asians inside Uzbekistan. Many of these nonindigenous people—mostly Russians but also Ukrainians, Germans, Koreans, and Turks—had been forcibly exiled to Uzbekistan. Others had been moved there to assist in Soviet development schemes, such as military manufacturing during World War II or the rebuilding of Tashkent after the terrible 1966 earthquake destroyed much of the city. In making this break, however, the Russians invited unintended consequences.

Russians and Ukrainians held many important and lucrative bureaucratic posts in Soviet Tashkent, Uzbekistan's capital. Typically, they served in the second- and third-level positions, just below the very visible Uzbek leader of Uzbekistan's Communist Party and just out of public sight. They also held authority as factory and collective farm managers and in the important provincial water ministries. With independence, opportunities for advancement started to shift in favor of the Uzbeks, and a pattern sometimes called "Uzbekization" started to take shape. In recent years, Russians have been confronted with regional and even violent protests against their old ruling status. They have watched the systematic de-Russification of street names, literature, and history curricula. They have been stung by the Uzbek Language Law of 1989, by an eruption of Islam across their formerly Orthodox-dominant territories, and by the government of Uzbekistan's rejection of dual citizenship. The Russians, formerly a favored group, have therefore been evacuating Uzbekistan. From 13 percent of the population in 1979, they dropped to 4 percent in 1999.

Uzbeks regard themselves as *Sarts* (settled people), in contrast to the nomadic peoples of neighboring Kazakhstan, Kyrgyzstan, or Turkmenistan. As such, the Uzbeks take pride in their great and ancient cities. Tashkent was the fourth-largest city in the USSR, and today it has a population of about 2.3 million. Samarkand has a population of almost 500,000, and Bukhara's population is 250,000. In the Fergana Valley, Namangan and Andijon each have about 300,000 people, with Kokand and Farghona following at about 200,000 each. Even so, 80 percent of all Uzbekistanis—18 million people—live in rural towns and collective farm villages. It is here that we most clearly see the fabric of Uzbekistan's society.

EDUCATION

In order to develop a trained work force, the Soviet Union sought to educate its citizens. It is also worth remembering that all media in the USSR were censored and used to broadcast the government's message. It was, for purpose of spreading propaganda, an official priority that people read. In Uzbekistan, practically everyone over the age of 20 is literate. Because the government still controls almost all print and broadcast news, literacy remains a high priority. There is also a long tradition of educating children in Uzbekistan, stemming from a history of trade and commerce as the midpoint of the Great Silk Road. Mass education, however, is a complicated and expensive process. Now that Moscow no longer provides financial assistance, Uzbekistan is struggling to assume this task.

To complicate things further, the government of Uzbekistan has ordered that Uzbek history and literature be taught and that it be taught in Uzbek. It also has ruled that written Uzbek change from the Cyrillic alphabet (the Russian alphabet used in all textbooks) to the Latin alphabet (used in most of the Western world). Without sizeable textbook budgets, adequate numbers of Uzbek-speaking teachers, or parents familiar with Latin script, however, these educational goals are not gaining traction. The government has shortened the period of required education from 11 years to 9, and it has called half of all elementary school buildings structurally unsuitable. The tradition of sending children out to pick cotton lives on in Uzbekistan, where schooling is interrupted for ten weeks every year at harvest time. The tight economy is now keeping even more children out of school altogether; many must help their parents at home and in the fields. Today, only about a third of high-school-aged people attend a secondary or vocational school.

There is a special respect for higher education in Uzbekistan, following the great medical, mathematical, and engineering accomplishments of ancient times. There are still 50 institutions of higher education operating in the country, but their budgets have been slashed since Soviet days, and professors increasingly work part time. Again, the withdrawal of Soviet support is acutely felt. Russian scientific research was advanced, but that connection is now severed. With it have gone many Russian technical instructors, important library acquisitions, laboratory supplies, publishing facilities, and research opportunities. Industrial, financial, and research sectors of the economy have also withered since independence. With a sharp decline in the number of highly skilled positions, there is less incentive to offer specialized and costly training. An authoritarian state, moreover, can result in a difficult learning environment. Environmental problems would seem to be an ideal issue for earth scientists to study in Uzbekistan. Unfortunately, the government, at every level, does not welcome challenges to established water policies or investigations of the economy. Soil surveys and groundwater studies, for instance, are not available for unauthorized access, and authorization is restricted to the authorities. To these barriers can be added a virtual absence of Internet access, a chronic lack of copy machines, and poor communication and data sharing between institutions. The ability of the academic community to produce scholars or to advance the economy is becoming problematic.

ALLEGIANCE

Observers in economically advanced democracies tend to think of countries as voluntary associations of people. Although the United States is uniquely flexible in this regard, most of us also tend to connect countries with a specific ethnic group, language, and religion—France with French people, Japan with the Japanese, Spain with the Spanish, and so on. Such associations do not attach firmly to Uzbekistan. The territory of Uzbekistan was carved out of Turkistan by a foreign colonizer, the USSR. In the nineteenth century, the Russian Empire assembled Turkistan from several small competing kingdoms. These kingdoms—the emirate of Bukhara and the khanates of Kokand and Khiva—had established patterns of identity and loyalty decades and even centuries before any thought was given to creating the Soviet central Asian republics. Those historic patterns of association live on today.

The most common social identification across Uzbekistan is with one's clan—a group with shared experience, a shared history, and a clear ethnic lineage. Clans are part of the greater tribal heritage, which is a primary bonding agent across the whole middle Asian region. Families in Uzbekistan are generally bigger than American families. They also live in closer proximity than is common in such mobile cultures as the United States and Western Europe. Sons, especially the oldest sons, rarely abandon their parents. Daughters, on the other hand, usually move away to raise families with other people's sons. For most citizens of Uzbekistan, home is a village or medium-sized town. Families live together in a compound or nearby, disbursed throughout the *mahalla,* or neighborhood. Families, clans, and tribes give individuals in Uzbekistan a sense of identity that some in wealthier and more distracted societies might envy. Unfortunately, the same formula for group cohesion prevents Uzbekistan from becoming a cohesive nation of laws and equal rights.

Uzbekistan owes its statehood to a Soviet reorganization of Turkistan in 1924. Further reforms in 1929 and 1936 created the current configuration of central Asian republics. Even as Soviet planners were elevating Uzbekistan's stature to a titular nationality (a nationality with its own named republic), however, other policies were created to weaken the Uzbeks and frustrate any tendency to real nationalism. The Communist Party was an atheist institution, and early in the life of Uzbekistan, Islamic expression was severely limited and discouraged by the government. In this way, it was thought, religious ties would become little more than a bit of folklore in the average Uzbekistani's life experience.

Between 1928 and 1933, mosques all across central Asia were closed. Their number fell from 26,000 to fewer than 100. Muslim Uzbeks were drafted into the army, but they were rarely trusted in important positions and usually spent their time performing free labor elsewhere in the USSR. Limited numbers of Muslim clerics were allowed to practice and write, but their work was monitored and edited by state authorities so that it painted the Soviet Union as a friend of Islam. In this way, the

Because the Communist Party suppressed religious belief and expression, many people were forced to secretly practice their faith. Today, religious expression is allowed and is emerging from private homes into the open. These Uzbek Muslims are worshipping together in Tashkent in 2001.

USSR hoped to be seen as an attractive model to Muslim populations beyond the new empire, and Soviet ideals and relations might spread. This pretense of honoring Islam gained some traction among other dictatorial regimes in southwest Asia, as among the Baathist Parties in Syria and Iraq. Most Muslims, however, never believed that the Soviet Union was their friend.

In 1929, the Uzbek alphabet was changed from Arabic to Latin (like the letters you are reading now). This prevented most Uzbeks from reading their own history or celebrating their own rich literature. It also allowed the schools to teach Uzbek children a fictional account of the Soviet generosity toward Uzbekistan—an important step in the attempt to "Russify" the culture of the country. As elsewhere in the USSR, authorities instructed children to report attempts by their parents to teach anything contrary to the official history. In the process of rewriting facts for the glorification of the ruling regime, the Soviet Communist Party was practicing a type of propaganda called "historiography."

In the 1930s, almost all of the talented and recognized Uzbek writers were rounded up and killed, and a new class of writers was trained to write in service to Communist Party ideals. This, of course, further distanced the Uzbeks from their own collective identity. Russian became the only language of advancement in government, science, industry, or the military. Steadily, Russian words were injected into the Uzbek vocabulary. All children learned Russian in school, and the most promising young minds were promoted to studies elsewhere in the Soviet Union, usually Russia. In 1937, the Uzbek leadership was accused of holding nationalist (and therefore separatist) tendencies, and all were killed. In 1939, the Cyrillic alphabet (the alphabet used by Russians and other Slavs) was adopted in Uzbekistan and the Latin alphabet was abandoned. This gave the Moscow planners and party officials another chance to sanitize the official "truth" of the Uzbek experience.

Uzbekistan is now more than 80 percent Uzbek, up from 70 percent in 1992. Just as Uzbekization has affected the Russians and Ukrainians living in the country, it also affects other non-Uzbek central Asians as well. Since 1992, opportunities for Uzbeks—so long a second-class group in their own republic—have been increasing and opportunities for other groups have declined. Uzbekistan's other minority central

Asians include Tajiks, with at least 5 percent of the total population, and Kazakhs and Karakalpaks, with about 4 percent each. The number of Tajks is uncertain; when Uzbekistan was created in 1924, the Tajik cities of Bukhara and Samarkand were included in order to weaken ethnic nationalism among all groups involved. Ever since that time, the Tajiks in these cities have been officially Uzbek; Uzbekization now discourages anyone from disputing that.

Whether or not it is their traditional ethnic language, more Uzbekistanis are now learning Uzbek. Historically, Kazakhs, Kyrgyz, and Karakalpaks were nomadic groups, so they are largely dismissed by the Uzbek Sarts. These people might all be moderate Muslims and mostly farmers and ranchers. They might all be Turkic-Mongols and mostly contemptuous of Russians. In clan societies, however, it is differences that define people. Uzbeks are a hospitable people, but few of them would welcome a Kazakh, a Kyrgyz, or a Russian into their family.

Recognition of a unique Uzbek culture rests on many traits. As a rural people, Uzbeks were excluded from access to material wealth and power, but their isolation also contributed to their never having been stripped of their culture. They wore embroidered skullcaps rather than Russian brimmed hats. They always removed their shoes when entering a home. They never drank vodka, and their tea was the Oriental green variety not the black European favorite. Their bread, called *nan,* is not shaped into loaves but is round and flat and regarded almost reverently. Stale or excess nan is perched on a fencepost or stair railing and never dropped on the ground or lain upside down. Moreover, despite their forced production of cotton, they found ways to supply themselves with a variety of fresh fruits, vegetables, and melons while the Russians ate primarily potatoes.

Because they were so far from Moscow, they managed to secretly practice Islam, and their jokes about the Soviet leadership were not so hushed. Their families were not broken

A man buys bread from a street vendor at a market in Termez near the Afghan and Uzbek border. This round flat bread is a staple in the diet of the Uzbek people.

up to serve in some Siberian industrial project thousands of miles away. Their most important holiday has remained *Nouvruz* (the first day of spring) and not the first of January as it is for the Russians. In reality, a different standard of wealth replaced professional opportunity or the acquisition of material things in Uzbekistan, and it still does. Wealth is measured in the joy of a large family, in close friends with plenty of time for visiting, in the communal disciplines of Islam, respect for old people, compassion for the infirm, and in patient and gentle conversation.

With the fall of the USSR, Islam is reemerging from private homes and asserting itself as the universalizing experience

Attendance at mosques has risen in recent years and the number of students attending *madrassas*, such as this one in Bukhara, has increased as well.

across all of formerly Soviet central Asia. Within Uzbekistan, a gradual and steady movement is reflected in hundreds of rehabilitated mosques. Attendance at these mosques is rising, student attendance at *madrassas* (Islamic schools) is growing, and an Islamic political movement is increasing in strength—especially in the youthful, crowded, and underemployed cities of the Fergana Valley. Friday prayers are well attended, periods of fasting are more widely recognized, increasing numbers of Uzbeks and Tajiks are making the *hajj* (pilgrimage) to Mecca, and young intellectuals are studying Arabic—the language of the Koran. Uzbekistan's state leadership, itself a holdover from atheist days, has expressed concern that Islam might eclipse the state as a principal unifier and motivator among the population. Those government expressions will be examined more closely in the next chapter. For now, it is important to remember that Uzbekistan's population is 88 percent Muslim, mostly of the Sunni branch of Islam, and that Uzbekistan is home to a number of significant Muslim landmarks and an important school of Islamic thought.

5

Government

Decisions and authority in Uzbekistan filter down from the capital, Tashkent, and mostly from the president through provincial governments called *hokimiats*. Each of Uzbekistan's 12 provinces is governed by a *hokim* (like a state governor) who has been appointed and can be replaced by the president. Interests and influence work their way upward through the hokimiat by the force of regional power lobbies rooted in clans. Clans in Uzbekistan are geographically concentrated, connected through extended family ties. They tend to specialize in particular vocations. The hokim is sensitive to the skills and needs of larger clans. The president of Uzbekistan appoints a prime minister and deputy prime ministers who are responsible for overseeing agriculture, energy, trade and transportation, as well as culture, education, health, and labor. All of these people answer to the president.

The current president of Uzbekistan, Islam Karimov, is passionate about tennis and in 2001 took part in the awards ceremony for the President's Tennis Cup in Tashkent.

In the Soviet era, the Communist Party placed hard demands on workers and the environment, so the people of Uzbekistan are used to authoritarian leadership. When Uzbekistan became independent in 1991, the Party leadership clung to power, keeping the entrenched political chain of economic command in place. One change, however, involved renaming the Communist Party of Uzbekistan—it became the Peoples' Democratic Party of Uzbekistan. The leadership promised free and fair elections, but this change has not materialized. Press censorship is now officially unconstitutional, but government domination of the news media is still virtually complete. Journalists who write articles that the government finds offensive are often harassed and even arrested.

The judicial branch of government minds the executive branch. Officially, competitive political parties are now the law of the land, but the legislature meets only a few days each year, and all political parties in the legislature support the president and his policies. Soviet police-state tactics have been renounced, but the United Nations still condemns the "systemic use" of torture in Uzbekistan. Political opponents of President Karimov have been exiled and even hunted in foreign countries. The government has privatized Soviet-era collective farms, but as yet little has changed. Lack of significant change can also be seen in the ecology lottery. Proceeds from this gambling game were supposed to correct environmental problems, but this has not occurred. In fact, after more than a decade of independence and some cosmetic tinkering, very few changes have altered domestic politics.

Clearly, unquestioned central rule is an accepted norm in Uzbekistan. For many reasons, this is not at all surprising. When independence was thrust on Uzbekistan in 1991, the republic's leadership decided to enact a "state nationalism" program—promoting allegiance to Uzbekistan. To citizens of mature democratic countries, this exercise might seem almost pointless. In established democracies, it is natural for most citizens to pledge allegiance to their country of birth or selection. This does not necessarily happen in countries where independence is new, particularly if independence came about as it did in Uzbekistan.

Uzbekistan, for example, was not a country for which anyone fought a revolution. It was formed to serve specific purposes for the Soviet Union, the greatest of which was to produce raw cotton. Its borders do not naturally conform to the distribution of Uzbek people. Its independence was not demanded or even widely celebrated. There is little sense of broad unity or universal purpose among the country's citizens.

For all of these reasons, Uzbekistan's independence meant facing the very real possibility that the republic could simply dissolve. In order to avert chaos and to maintain its own control over the economy, the country's leadership was suddenly given the task of reinforcing the identity and mission of Uzbekistan. This is no small challenge, considering the forces that are at work in the country. In Uzbekistan, there are three levels of national consciousness. The first of these levels is subnationalism, based on the *mahalla* (neighborhood), on clans, and on popular identifications with the historic kingdoms, especially Kokand, Bukhara, and Khiva. The second level is state nationalism, which champions official interpretations of the Uzbek bloodline, Uzbek language, and the glory of past rulers such as Timur. It is unfortunate for the state leadership that this middle level is the weakest. The third level, supranationalism, is based on association with old Turkistan and especially with a greater community of Turkish speakers that includes Turks, Uzbeks, Kazakhs, Turkmen, Kyrgyz, Azeris, and even the Uighurs of western China. It is also based on the strongest of supranational attractions—Islam.

The challenge of inspiring the populace to pledge allegiance to Uzbekistan is formidable. Only if the people can be convinced that the state government represents their aspirations, upholds their heritage, and protects their material well being, can sub- and supranationalism weaken under the weight of public self-interest. The government's campaign to build state nationalism appears to be utilizing four main tools and several auxiliary incentives.

The first of these tools is glorifying the accomplishments and stature of President Karimov and tying him closely to the state's identity. This act of linking is reminiscent of the infamous "cult of personality" and is used often in situations of "strongman rule." A culture that has produced great khans and has survived a brutal Communist regime has ample experience with strong rule: It is, after all, what the people have known. Revolutionary leaders, moreover, are frequently drawn to this tool of leadership. In some cases, they find it attractive because their vision for the new state is still in the design stage. In other cases, they do not trust the people to run the country through grassroots institutions. In the case of Uzbekistan, President Karimov is a leader trained in totalitarian methods. He is leading people who have no experience with the opportunities or responsibilities that accompany independence. He is formulating domestic and foreign policies practically single-handedly. President Karimov is the unchallenged star of television news. Every day, he is shown in meetings, greeting dignitaries, delivering speeches, writing his programs, signing agreements, and traveling around the country. People expect nothing less than a complete leader, and his ability to deliver that image is synonymous with the efficacy of Uzbekistan. Even his past activities are shown and reshown, sometimes with stirring background music and often without reference to when the activities took place. It is sometimes difficult to believe that one man can stay so busy.

The government's second tool is historiography. Historiography is the rewriting of history in order to unify the public behind heroic feats from the past. All nations romanticize their past, but historiography is a step beyond embellishment and includes propaganda. Certainly the elevation of President Karimov to a superman-type figure is a sort of contemporary historiography. Another example is the rehabilitation of past leaders whose unsavory deeds are cleansed or whitewashed for the specific purpose of "improving" the image of the past.

For a traditional model of historiography, we need only to consider the makeover of Timur of Samarkand. In truth, Timur spent his life (1336–1405) savagely conquering innocent people. *Timur* (a name he chose for himself) means "Man of Iron." The conqueror claimed a bloodline kinship to Genghis Khan (which may or may not have been true). When Timur was still in his 20s, his right leg and arm were badly injured in battle, so he became known as "Timur-the-Lame" (Tamerlane). He presided over the glorification of Samarkand but in all likelihood was rarely there. In 1398, he invaded India, massacred the entire population

The Emir Timur Square in Tashkent boasts a huge statue of Timur (Tamerlane), who was a famous but brutal conqueror who claimed kinship with Genghis Khan.

of Delhi, destroyed everything in his path, and built towers from 100,000 of his victims' skulls. In 1401, he took Damascus, slaughtering 20,000 people. Nations far beyond his control, including Egypt, paid him tribute—a bribe to stay away! Timur is believed to have killed 17 million people. He was a brutal conqueror and a terrible ruler. He built no societies, helped no one, and improved nothing.

Suddenly, in the interest of promoting state nationalism, his brutal history is forgotten. In the center of Tashkent is Emir Timur Square. This square's name has changed ten times during the past century in order to accommodate the preferred hero of the day. Today, it boasts a huge statue of Timur—riding a great stallion, in command, right arm outstretched, with no lameness. On the monument is inscribed "My Strength is in Justice." Thus, with a historiographic makeover, Timur has a

The Emir Timur Museum houses exhibits devoted to the history of the fourteenth-century conqueror Timur, as will as the long history of Uzbekistan.

new image. Tashkent's new Emir Timur Museum makes the point that he brought glory to Samarkand and to Uzbekistan (nonexistent at that time) through intelligence and moral clarity. Sick people claim that his tomb exudes healing powers, and newlyweds visit his statues for good luck. To this museum, President Karimov has contributed this observation: "The figure of our forefather Emir Timur surely symbolizes the pride and honor of our people." With the cleansing of Timur's reputation, moreover, Karimov himself gains serious latitude in his own treatment of political opponents.

The third tool used to enhance state nationalism is the endorsement of Sufiism. Sufiism is an esteemed sect of the

Islamic faith, and Uzbekistan is thought to be the birthplace of the Sufi-Muslim tradition. To ward off imported or pan-regional Islamic movements, the state has embraced the Uzbeks' and Tajiks' own homegrown religious tradition. In so doing, it seeks to strengthen its own moral underpinning and political legitimacy. President Karimov is, of course, aware of the destabilizing power of radical Islamic movements, and he has frequently expressed his loathing for political Islam. Uzbekistan shares a border with Afghanistan, so the Taliban revolution presented an immediate threat to Uzbekistan's secular government, as have recent Islam-centered conflicts in Tajikistan, Pakistan, Kashmir, and Uighurstan (western China). In 1999, a series of terrorist bombings in Tashkent killed at least a dozen people. Karimov quickly blamed Islamic extremists. He accused them of seeking to destabilize the country and kill the president; a big crackdown followed, with widespread rumors of torture.

At the same time, the president is aware that religion runs far deeper through the history of the Uzbeks than does a state called Uzbekistan. He must be careful not to alienate his own people. From his earlier role as a committed Communist and atheist leader, he has now assumed the role of a pious believer. He has traveled to Mecca for the *hajj* (pilgrimage) and has taken the oath of office with his right hand on the Koran. Government-controlled bookstores (all bookstores) have been stocked with a large supply of Sufi manuals detailing where and when Sufiism began, how it is practiced, and how it differs from other, alien Islamic sects.

Most citizens of Uzbekistan are not politically active, and they do not tend to expect political action through Islam. Today, however, many young people are underemployed and deeply frustrated by the absence of economic opportunities or the freedom to speak out. There is now growing concern that they might rally around the one movement that has been angrily and repeatedly condemned by the state leadership—

political Islam. Indeed, despite governmental controls over the media, information streams in. The global Islamic movement is well known to Uzbek intellectuals, and they commonly and patiently confide that "the Koran will beat Karimov." The government has banned the Islamic Movement of Uzbekistan because of its incendiary rhetoric. In the Fergana Valley, the main mosque of Andijon was closed after its chief cleric called on Uzbeks to embrace revolutionary Islam. His audiotapes now circulate secretly.

A fourth tool used to promote state nationalism is a policy aimed at keeping the clans on board. Because the clan remains the basic social connection in Uzbekistan, the government strengthens itself and the state system by strengthening ties between itself and the clans. This is done by promoting local clan leaders to positions of authority in the government and by distributing favor to the provincial hokims, who maintain strong ties to local clan elders. In this way, the government in Tashkent cultivates genuine familial ties between itself and the people.

For centuries, central Asia was effectively governed through the clan network and clan leaders held power through a disciplined feudal hierarchy. The old khanates of Khiva (subjugated by the Russian Empire in 1873), Kokand (which lost power in 1878), and Bukhara (which became part of the Soviet Union in 1922) historically fought among themselves. Each one joined with Russia and the USSR under the best terms that it could muster at the time, and none willingly succumbed to the guidance of Tashkent. President Karimov's apparent model for clan governance is Sharaf Rashidov, the Communist Party boss of the Uzbek Soviet Socialist Republic between 1959 and 1983. Rashidov was a master of patronage, appointing faithful clan leaders from different provinces to fill important government positions. In this way, favors were dispensed according to a chain of loyalties, whole clans gained prestige, and the state ruler was transformed into a beloved godfather.

One form of public diversion that has been enhanced by independence and serves as another government tool for promoting nationalism is sports. In the Communist USSR, tennis was rejected as a dalliance of the capitalist country-club class, so (together with golf) it was practically nonexistent. In today's Uzbekistan, tennis is seen as a means of providing young people with an alternative to the emerging interest in Islam. Islam is austere; tennis is entertaining, and the government does its best to capitalize on this distinction. Since the mid-1990s, the government has built more than 400 tennis courts across Uzbekistan. Provincial politicians are taking up the game, and with good reason—it happens to be President Karimov's favorite. The press has lavished coverage on Uzbekistan's own Iroda Tulyaganova, ranked thirty-ninth among all women tennis players by the World Tennis Association in 2003, another way of fostering national pride.

CHAPTER

6

Uzbekistan's Economy

C ertainly Uzbekistan's greatest resource—employing the most people and generating the most revenue—is its ability to support agriculture. Forty-four percent of the population works in agriculture, and 62 percent of Uzbekistan's total area is used for some sort of crop or livestock production. These are very high percentages by world standards. The government has announced its intention to shift cropping away from cotton in order to achieve self-sufficiency in grains. This, however, seems to be a very gradual move, and 40 percent of Uzbekistan's total hard currency income still comes from the sale of cotton. This makes the economy vulnerable to fluctuations in market demand for and world pricing of cotton. There are signs, however, that suggest a different future for Uzbekistan's agricultural economy.

Uzbekistan is famous for its quality fruits and vegetables, and the immediate region is home to 40 million people, all of whom must

Forty percent of Uzbekistan's hard currency income comes from the sale of cotton. These students are picking cotton, or "white gold," in the town of Termez, which lies close to the border with Afghanistan.

eat. Most fruit and vegetable crops consume less water and could bring higher prices than cotton to the average Uzbek farm worker. Demand for food surely will be rising with the regional population. Unfortunately, perishable food crops also expose weaknesses in Uzbekistan's transportation, storage, and food processing systems, all of which are inadequate.

Since independence, there have been terrific discoveries of oil and natural gas, making it possible for Uzbekistan to eliminate oil imports and generate gas exports. For the foreseeable future, Uzbekistan will be able to provide its own fuel needs and also increase its energy exports. Other sources of wealth include a rich gold deposit at Murantau, which produces 60 tons of bullion annually, ranking Uzbekistan ninth among countries in the production of this precious metal. During the Soviet era, Uzbekistan's gold was exploited for the enrichment of the Soviet government in Moscow; most Uzbeks didn't even know it existed until they gained independence. There are also marketable uranium, silver, and copper reserves. In total, the country is thought to have $13 trillion worth of resources in the ground. Uzbekistan manufactures automobiles and aircraft and has mechanical engineering plants, textile factories, and a diverse building materials industry. Economic growth is also supported by a system of state universities and libraries.

REACHING OUT

In order to sell its wealth—whether grown, mined, or manufactured—Uzbekistan needs access to the world market, specifically a market able to pay in hard (universally tradable) currency. In order to sell its newly discovered oil and gas, Uzbekistan will need a pipeline to an ocean port. This presents a great challenge. To say that Uzbekistan is landlocked understates its predicament, because it is one of only two doubly landlocked countries in the world (Lichtenstein is the only other country that is separated from an ocean by two other countries). This level of isolation makes Uzbekistan vulnerable to the economic and political misfortunes of surrounding countries. Fortunately, it also affords those neighbors an opportunity to help themselves by helping Uzbekistan.

The best-positioned country to benefit from Uzbek trade is Afghanistan. In fact, one of the opportunities that came when the Taliban regime was overthrown by U.S. forces in 2002 was for a unified and stable Afghanistan to construct a rail-highway-pipeline corridor to Pakistan and on to the Indian Ocean, perhaps reaching energy-starved India. Such a project could generate wealth for all participants and would encourage each of the countries involved to invest in the prosperity of the others. No country would benefit more than Uzbekistan, a place with a positive image throughout southern Asia. Unfortunately, Afghanistan is neither unified nor stable at the present time, so this dream remains on hold.

With the fall of the Soviet Union, many strategic analysts expected central Asia to attract foreign intrigue reminiscent of the Great Game played by Russia and England. The obvious states to watch for this kind of involvement are Turkey and Iran. Turkey, of course, shares linguistic and ethnic roots with the Uzbek people and struggles with its isolation from European nations, from Russia, and from the Arab states. The newly independent countries of central Asia have presented Turkey with an opportunity for cultivating cultural, economic, and military alliances. This is happening, but very slowly. In seeking such positive alliances, Turkey learned early that Uzbekistan was not looking for a new "big brother" to replace Russia. Other neighborhood states, namely Russia, Iran, and Armenia, also worry about an aggressive Turkish foreign policy, so the Turkish government has prudently given them little to worry about.

Iran is another state from which watchers of central Asia could expect an assertive foreign policy. Iranian Persians are also isolated from the Arabs and from India, the colossus of southern Asia. Despite Iran's proximity to Turkmenistan and Uzbekistan and the easy access it can offer to the Persian Gulf, there is a real language barrier between these subregions of middle Asia. Few central Asian Muslims are of the Persians' Shiia sect. Furthermore, the Uzbek leadership is very cautious about closing ranks with a theocratic state such as the Islamic Republic of Iran, and so this connection remains tentative.

ECONOMIC STRATIFICATION

In the United States or Western Europe, we are generally satisfied to view an economy in abstract terms: Gross Domestic Product per capita or (for those countries with transnational corporations) Gross National Product per capita. Uzbekistan's economic viewpoint is very different. Although many Uzbekistanis would be considered part of the "middle class," working their way up through the system, many more have effectively opted out. These workers—perhaps 5 million of them, together with their families—live in rural villages of 500 or fewer or in medium-sized towns of 10,000 to 20,000; the majority work in agriculture at least part of the time.

The *kolkhoz* (collective farm) is the main productive enterprise of the village and the main employer of village residents. These large farms were assembled from smaller private farms in the 1930s because the Soviet Union was founded on the ideal of disowning the individual in order to enrich society as a whole. The purpose of agriculture, it was thought, should be to feed and clothe the urban workers and soldiers so that the USSR could become powerful in terms of heavy industry and military power. The practice worked for a few decades, but it starved the farms for investments and kept the villagers very poor. Indeed, during the Soviet era and even today, the Uzbek *dekan* (peasant farmworker) was and is essentially just getting by.

Since the early 1990s, collective farms in Uzbekistan have been "reformed," and all the kolkhoz workers are supposed to be part owners, permitted to grow whatever they want. That, at least, is the theory. In fact, the kolkhoz is still run by a kolkhoz manager, who also serves as mayor and general manager of the village. He occupies the honored seat at most community weddings, advises parents on raising their children, and commands respect for his power to provide or deny irrigation water, seed, and fertilizer. He can accept or refuse a farmer's harvest. New lands in the expanding *kolkhozi* (collective farms) are leased to dekans who apply for them. In spite of theoretical policy, the best land in the kolkhoz is still dedicated to cotton. Priority for irrigation water goes to cotton, and when the villagers go to work on the kolkhoz, the crop they usually farm is cotton because it is the crop the government in Tashkent demands. Clearly, cotton is still "King" in Uzbekistan.

At home, peasants and villagers have ample opportunity to cultivate their own private gardens. These gardens yield a substantial share of villagers' food. Self-sufficiency and bartering and selling at the local open-air bazaar (the most popular form

Rows of spice vendors compete at the Chorsu Market in Tashkent. These open-air bazaars are a very popular form of marketplace in the country.

of marketplace) have become mainstays of the local economies. Many rural farmers own cars and telephones, but subsidies from Moscow for fuel and utilities are a fading memory since independence. In place of the old system, most *kolkhozniki* (collective farmworkers) are now simply going without. Throughout the villages of Uzbekistan, there are telephones that do not work, cars that will not run, and people who never travel, simply because the kolkhozniki operate in a virtually cashless economy. Their stories, therefore, are not told in the economic statistics with which we are so familiar in the postindustrialized West.

Others—perhaps one and a half million teachers, drivers, craftsmen, and shopkeepers with modest cash-paying jobs—

live with their families in a dozen larger cities. During the Soviet era, cities received a sporadic stream of consumer goods, including car parts, refrigerators, furniture, and toys, all of irregular quality. Now, city residents shop the bazaars and window-shop at their local department stores for light bulbs and shoes, towels and bicycle parts, TV tubes, toothpaste, or maybe even a musical instrument. The lucky few drive cars, but most ride the bus. They send their children to public school and pay small fees for electricity and haphazard telephone service.

Middle-class city dwellers used to pay rent, but now their standardized Soviet block apartments have mostly been privatized. Although this saves money, the buildings are not well cared for. These middle-class families depend on the ability of the government to export and sell cotton or minerals at good prices, to attract foreign aid, or to accommodate foreign investment in stores or light manufacturing inside their cities. Most say that they were materially better off under the Soviet Union. These people do use cash, and they are sensitive to the government's periodic revaluation of Uzbek currency, the standard unit of which is the *sum*. The sum's value has drifted downward as the government has sought to make its exports more attractive to foreign buyers. A more accurate rate is found in the black market, where Uzbeks pay 30 and 40 percent more sum for each dollar.

Higher in the pecking order are tens of thousands at the top of Uzbekistan's ruling political class, who typically prosper from their strong concentration of power. Most of these elite are former Communist Party officers who have retained their privileged positions. They raise their families in Tashkent, the most modern city in the country. They drive their own cars, usually the better Russian-made models or imports. They see dentists, smoke American cigarettes, and vacation abroad. Their teenage children have cell phones and buy luxury goods in foreign shops. These people can afford to eat meat every night.

POLITICAL CONSEQUENCES OF ECONOMIC DECISIONS

From the earliest periods of settlement—perhaps 6,000 years ago—people of the region recognized the central role of water in their lives. In Bukhara and Samarkand, societies developed around the protection and manipulation of water. Under Islamic law, the head of state—the emir or the khan—retained sovereignty over lands and waters. Historically, individual farmers controlled and worked the same plots of land for generations, but water was provided by the state. In this way, agricultural management became a government concern, with little real control being held by small-scale operators. Little has changed in this regard.

In the late 1800s, the Russian tsars conquered central Asia and set about transforming it into a cotton supply base for their empire. This scheme was driven in part by the American Civil War, during which the blockade on cotton sales from the Southern states exposed Russia's dependence on cotton imports. Russia's response to losing cotton imports from the South was to create an alternative source of cotton. Russians reconstructed old dams across rivers, filled reservoirs, and dug 50 large *ariqs* (canals) through the Fergana Valley, over the Goladnaya Steppe, on the Amu Darya Delta, and parallel to the Zeravshan River. All of the most important Central Asian installations were placed on territories of today's Uzbekistan. The Russian Empire forced this land farther and farther into the task of growing cotton. Cotton deliveries rose 500 percent between 1899 and 1907. Grain crops were replaced by cotton, and food self-sufficiency gave way to a dependence on food from other regions of the empire. In this way, Uzbekistan's cotton growing potential was maximized for the benefit of the controlling power in Moscow; any chances for economic or political independence for Uzbekistan were minimized.

NO RELIEF

In 1917, the Russian Empire was overthrown, and in its place emerged the Communist empire of the USSR. The only change this brought to Uzbekistan was an acceleration of the cottonization strategy. Some of the earliest Soviet decrees commanded increased cotton production. Ironically, such demands came at a time when the new regime was fighting a brutal civil war against Uzbeks and dozens of other ethnic groups wanting to break free of Russian and Bolshevik domination. In the end, the civil war failed to stop the Communists, and Soviet agricultural strategy for Uzbekistan was enforced.

According to the Soviet model, economic development would be pushed relentlessly along by demanding "Five-year Plans." The most advertised in this series of plans, and commonly thought to be the first, was that assigned to heavy industry for the period between 1928 and 1933. But the first five-year cotton plan was actually begun in 1922, six years earlier. Between 1924 and 1926, water management decisions were removed from local control and assumed by central authorities in Moscow. Collectivization of agriculture in the 1920s and 1930s was ruthlessly advanced across the lands of Uzbekistan. Cotton requisitions in the 1920s, for example, left Uzbeks and other regional peasants without enough cotton for their own clothing or for mattresses to sleep on.

By 1928, cotton covered almost 40 percent of all irrigated land in Soviet Uzbekistan, rising to 56 percent by 1932. Established irrigation "norms" were soon raised by an additional 30 percent to accommodate the spread of cotton, and a railroad connection was made to the Trans-Siberian Line in 1930 for transportation of the huge cotton harvests. World War II preoccupied the Moscow planners as the Soviet Union fought for its life against the invading German army. Uzbek farmers took advantage of the distraction, replacing some of the cotton crops with food. This came to an end in June 1945—barely a month after the war's end—when Moscow ordered the immediate restoration and increased production of cotton in Uzbekistan.

Raw cotton from Uzbekistan clothed the Russian and Soviet armies for the better part of a century. As demand grew, Uzbekistan's cotton fields were constantly expanded, and new lands were pressed into service. Uzbekistan's controlling resource, water, made it all possible. Water installations were steadily rebuilt, enlarged, and extended so that in the 1970s, water developments in Uzbekistan consumed most of the water budget for the entire USSR. Moreover, such large-scale water diversions fostered rivalries between upstream clans and midstream clans, with downstream groups increasingly denied adequate and clean water. Such rivalries further enhanced Moscow's power over granting regional allotments and arbitrating regional disputes.

In the late 1950s, a popular view in Moscow was that Uzbekistan's agriculture was draining the Soviet budget. There were also concerns that Central Asians were restoring their Muslim cities with Russian Orthodox technology. The then leader of the Soviet Union, General Secretary Khrushchev, even complained that cotton pickers were not working very hard for their pay. This was not true. Cotton picking is very hard work, and pickers suffered unhealthy exposure to poisonous chemicals. Meanwhile, a steady stream of Russification attacked Uzbek culture. Uzbeks could not hope to attain positions of power in Moscow, and the Soviet system was managing the leadership in their own capital of Tashkent. Uzbekistan's cotton production was overwhelmingly for export rather than for local use. Food and even fiber production had been sacrificed for the cotton monoculture (growth of a single crop). Gradually, many negative effects of cottonization began to wear on the environment. After ginning and baling, 90 percent of all central Asian cotton was woven in Russian mills (primarily near Moscow), so employment and productivity in the Soviet garment industry were dependent on a stream of raw cotton (two-thirds of which came from Uzbekistan). In addition, more than a third of Soviet cotton was exported to client states allied with the Soviet Union or into the world market—all for considerations paid to Moscow.

Life in Moscow was hard as well, so it was easy for people living there to believe that people elsewhere had it better. The impression was cultivated that central Asians had an easy time in the sun, whereas Slavic peoples to the north hammered out their lives in the dangerous mines and factories of Russia and Ukraine. For decades, decisions forced on Uzbekistan by Moscow were tinted by a hint of revenge. Thus, economic or environmental exploitation could be forgiven. From collectivization onward, Moscow's official behavior toward Uzbekistan suggested a plantation strategy.

In the late 1950s and early 1960s, the Soviet leadership proposed to introduce modernization to agriculture in Uzbekistan and elsewhere in the Soviet Union. Most Uzbeks were pleased with the idea. It was suggested that mechanization and chemical crop additives would pull Central Asia out of the fifteenth century and into the twentieth century in one leap. For its international image, the Soviet Union would look like a model caretaker of lesser-developed peoples. It would also be responding decisively to recent agricultural advances, collectively called the Green Revolution, emerging from Western Europe and the United States. For the Communist Party, celebrating these progressive policies was a growth industry. The *Encyclopedia of Cotton Growing* boasted, "For the Soviet period in Uzbekistan, there has been a strong, highly mechanized, intensive agriculture specializing in cotton production."

It could all be made to look rather good, but the purpose of Moscow's modernization program was, of course, only to extract more cotton. Even as production rose, the five-year plan targets rose faster. The cotton harvests kept pace or at least were reported to do so. It is worthwhile to note that by the 1970s, Uzbekistan was producing cotton almost exclusively for Moscow, seemingly without complaint. In retrospect, however, we can see that cultivating subsidies for cotton, machinery, and water installations from Moscow had become a very profitable enterprise for the Uzbek *nomenclatura*—an elite class of Uzbek

Communist Party bosses, water managers, provincial cotton handlers, and kolkhoz chairmen. It is not entirely surprising that this favored population was mostly Uzbek. Moscow had learned through the horrors of collectivization that non-Russians would cooperate more willingly under a policy called *khorenizatsia,* or nativization. Under this policy, ethnic Uzbeks would be placed in charge of local operations (with plenty of Russian advisors, of course), and Moscow would not meddle too deeply in clan-regional politics as long as the cotton came in. Moreover, Soviet cotton payments would trickle down through the Uzbek leadership structure, and Moscow would not interfere in small-scale private enterprises or black marketeering in the remote provinces of Uzbekistan. For kolkhoz managers and provincial party officials, payments, stipends, and subsidies funneled through well-worn channels. Kolkhoz managers could blame poverty on Moscow, and leaders in Tashkent held the faith of the public for their protection of khorenizatsia. In the remote parts of Uzbekistan—where most of the people of Uzbekistan lived—Soviet policies were practically ignored.

This arrangement continued until 1983. That year, it was discovered that cotton harvests were being consistently over-reported. Dirt was being thrown into the bins and water was hosed onto the cotton before weighing. Communist Party officials from the farms all the way to Tashkent and even in Moscow were implicated in a scheme to overbill the government and pocket the difference. This discovery initiated the infamous "cotton scandals" that continued to irritate relations between Moscow and Uzbekistan throughout the 1980s.

As it turned out, farm "modernization" neither gained adoption in Uzbekistan nor lessened the burden on the kolkhozniki. The introduction of farm machinery, especially mechanized cotton pickers, was not accompanied by adequate technical training. There was always a shortage of spare parts, mechanics, and even drivers, and it really did not serve Soviet interests to replace human cotton pickers on the thousands of kolkhozi anyway. Where would these peasants go, if not into the cities? Their job skills were not suitable for the city, and they would certainly aggravate demands for housing and services. Moreover, any Uzbekization of Tashkent would prompt a de-Russification of the capital city. For Moscow, as well as for the Uzbek elite, whose wealth derived from the smooth flow of subsidies down from Moscow and product up from the kolkhozi, this would not be good. Better than mechanical pickers, a more productive modernization would be the continued installation of large irrigation systems, so a weak mechanization policy was paired with a robust canal-digging program. This combination produced more cotton and no bothersome social changes. The legacy of such policies still exists. To this day, most Uzbek cotton is handpicked.

Another general promise of modernization not kept was that crop prices would rise. Throughout the Soviet era, one important means of getting the most cotton for the least money was that the price paid for cotton was always kept low. Agricultural reforms in 1959 brought an increase in prices paid for most crops in the USSR. For cotton, however, the price was actually lowered, supposedly to compensate for the never realized gains of mechanization. Again, in 1983, general crop price increases ignored cotton. From 1952 to 1988, wheat prices in the USSR rose 20 times. During the same period, cotton prices rose by two and a half times. Before the revolution, 2.2 pounds (one kilogram) of cotton bought an Uzbek peasant a cow. By the end of the Soviet era and the birth of Uzbek independence, a kilogram of cotton bought 15 boxes of matches. In 1988, the average income for Uzbekistanis was slightly more than half that of other residents of the USSR.

THE DIFFICULTY WITH CHANGING COURSE

Rather than a diversified agriculture for serving local economies and enriching the masses of Uzbekistan, a cotton monoculture was imposed on the people and land by decision makers in Moscow and Tashkent. Viewed from either of these capital cities, the negative fallout from cottonization was remote and quite tolerable, hidden as it was behind the veil of wealth that cotton crops provided. An important holdover from the Soviet era is that the short-term interests of the rulers are still separated from the long-term interests of the country. This legacy, together with Uzbekistan's enormous cotton infrastructure, will make decottonization very difficult.

For three generations, the people of Uzbekistan generally approved of what the Russians were doing to them. Later realizations that their lakes and rivers had been polluted, their great sea destroyed, their soils poisoned, and their people sickened came without surprise to the average citizen. There is, however, a problem that comes with acknowledging such facts, and that problem involves what to do about it. For Tashkent's power-brokers and their chain of command, cottonization appears to be what the Russians did *for* them, not *to* them. By all accounts, the Russians and Soviets had made the desert bloom. Drawing from just the two largest of Uzbekistan's rivers, let us consider the magnitude of these technical accomplishments.

Before leaving the Fergana Valley, the Syr Darya supplies huge volumes of water for valley canals. Digging of the Great Fergana Canal in 1939 was a heroic labor of intensity unsurpassed anywhere in the USSR: 160,000 collective farm workers with shovels dug 172 miles (274 kilometers) in 45 days. According to Ian M. Matley, "Even in the days of the Khans and the Begs, it is unlikely that such continuous pressure was ever applied to [the] local labor force." After passing through the Fergana Valley, the Syr irrigates both small- and large-scale farming operations through canals branching north toward Tashkent and into Kazakhstan's southernmost Chimkhent Province and south onto the *Golodnaya* (Hungry) Steppe. From these steppe developments, the Syr rolls onto the Kyzyl Kum (Red Desert) and ultimately runs toward the Syr Delta, but it no longer reaches the Aral Sea.

The Amu Darya pours out of the Tajik foothills and forms the border between Uzbekistan and Afghanistan. Soon after leaving that border, the Amu confronts a major diversion canal that draws water westward to flow along the north face of Turkmenistan's Kopet-Dagh (Dry Mountains). This enormous Kara Kum Canal was dug and filled with water from the Amu in the mid-1950s, and it quickly became the main water supply for Turkmenistan. In fact, Turkmenistan's population has grown even more quickly than that of Uzbekistan, and denying inflow to the Kara Kum Canal would be unthinkable. The canal has lengthened over ensuing years and has become the world's longest. Its withdrawals from the Amu have continued to grow; today, it draws about a quarter of the total Amu Darya away from its natural course. Slightly farther downslope, the Qarshi Steppe Canal diverts 1.44 cubic miles (6 cubic kilometers) annually. This is roughly equivalent to 14 percent of the water used in all of Canada. Farther on, the Amu is tapped for farming operations along a narrow path through a hundred miles of desert, before meeting the next fork in its road, the Amu-Bukhara Canal. Reminiscent of the Kara Kum Canal, farmlands around Bukhara have only begun drawing from the Amu in recent decades. Since 1963, however, the Bukhara and nearby Kara Kul oases have come to depend heavily on the Amu Darya, and withholding this water would now be impossible. Downstream another 150 miles (240 kilometers), the Amu branches off into numerous irrigation canals of Khwarazm Province and waters the ancient city of Khiva. These are some of central Asia's oldest irrigation canals, dating back 2,500 years, and a number of them were once navigable. After all of these diversions and more, it is apparent why only a few cubic miles reach the Aral Sea in any given year. Entering the 1990s, irrigation consumed fully 94 percent and 87 percent, respectively, of the Amu Darya and Syr Darya flows. Clearly, Uzbekistan's water crisis is an irrigation crisis.

The utility of Uzbekistan's farmland has long been expressed in terms of its cotton production: 864,600 tons

The Amu Darya pours out of the Tajik foothills and forms the border with Afghanistan. It is one of the major waterways in a country with a limited water supply.

(786,000 metric tons) in 1932 to 3.3 million tons (3 million metric tons) in 1956 and 5.83 million tons (5.3 million metric tons) reported in 1984. In the 1970s, Uzbekistan was producing about two-thirds of all Soviet cotton. In 1984, 62 percent of Uzbekistan's irrigated land was planted in cotton. By the end of the Soviet era, the Uzbek Republic, not quite 2 percent of the USSR's total area, accounted for 25 percent of all Soviet irrigated land. And cotton fields alone used 55 percent of all surface water entering the Aral Drainage Basin.

All of this looked good to the central planners, especially as Soviet resource accountants kept a peculiar set of books. Cotton was called "white gold" for its contribution to the economy, and irrigated cotton harvests took priority over land care. For development purposes in the USSR, only labor and capital had value for they were assets considered unavailable for other projects. Land and water had no value because they were considered limitless and assigned by the state without a market value. The USSR did, after all, cover 12 percent of Earth's land surface.

Now the Soviets are gone, and the government of Uzbekistan has called for a new "intensification" of agriculture. Uzbek planners, however, are still discounting the value of land and water resources from calculations of agricultural efficiency. Unfortunately, agricultural development in post-Soviet Uzbekistan has maintained the old course of extensive growth—plowing up more land, diverting more water, working land to exhaustion, and then moving on.

BARRIERS TO REFORM

Although the goals and policies of cottonization have been harmful to Uzbekistan's sustainable agriculture and practically fatal for the Aral Sea, redirecting this economy will be very difficult. It must be remembered that cotton is king in Uzbekistan. There is no comparably developed industry or employer, and there is no vigorous public debate on the problems associated with such an unbalanced dependence on one crop. In fact, many stubborn barriers hinder any attempt at agricultural reform in the country.

One of these barriers is a culture of excessive water consumption. In a diversified economy, money becomes the gauge of wealth. Where water is the controlling resource, control of water is the gauge of wealth. Water still has no market value in Uzbekistan. Today, it is owned and controlled by the government, just as in the past it was owned by the Soviet authorities, by the tsar's ambassador, and by the khan before that. Moreover, water installations have value but water does not. Therefore, local water agencies and kolkhozi benefit by demonstrating a perpetual need for water installations. The more water they use, the more development money, materials, and technology they can consume. Obviously, these institutions gain from wasting water. The following pattern emerges: Water consumption is unmeasured, leaky valves and pipes are everywhere, and farms operate on a "use it or lose it" principle. As a result, Uzbekistan loses much of its potential water supply. Much is lost by evaporation from flood irrigation practices, standing reservoirs, field drainage sumps, and unlined irrigation ditches. Some is lost from canal and storage basin seepage and healthy stands of thirsty weeds that grow in the ditches. More water is lost than is used to grow crops.

Another barrier to agricultural reform is the absence of private property and the weak sense of responsibility for the land. Consider the following: Cotton is very salt tolerant, so the suspension of soil salinity into the root zone (discussed earlier) does not necessarily rule out cotton farming. Cotton, in addition to being an extreme water consumer, consumes large amounts of soil nutrients and crop additives as well. Thus, cotton promotes rapid soil erosion and mineral depletion and contributes to serious water pollution problems because of its heavy utilization of pesticides, herbicides, and fertilizers. Alfalfa—a favorite rotation crop with cotton—uses even more water.

In contrast, wherever farmers own their own land, care of that land improves. Land-owning farmers monitor water and chemical applications more carefully, they level the land more exactly for uniform wetting of the soil, and they install drainage facilities to pull excess water away from the soil-root zone. The fruits of this labor are profits, and it follows that profit-driven (capitalist) economies generally produce better support for agriculture. Such support includes fast transportation, improved storage systems, and advanced food processing and packaging facilities.

An agricultural worker weighs cotton picked by children. All the processes involved in producing cotton for export are controlled by the government, so the drive to diversify is not encouraged.

Also improved are wholesale purchasing and distribution, banking and credit services, and competitive supplies of seed, feed, chemicals, technology, and information. Very little of this support exists today in Uzbekistan, and none of it is developing adequately for a sustainable agriculture to emerge.

There is little incentive for real change in Uzbekistan's primary economic sector because cotton empowers the central government. Cotton, after all, cannot be eaten or used on a significant scale by local peasants. It must be processed at regional gins, all of which are owned by the government. The only way to move it is on government-owned trucks and trains. The only way to sell it abroad for hard currency is through the government. The entire political network—from the top central administration down to the provincial hokimiats—is largely financed by the export of cotton. Its price to the kolkhoz is low, a few hundred dollars' worth of Uzbek money for each ton of processed cotton lint. Supplies of irrigation water are delivered to the kolkhozi by the district water ministries according to their usual and expected productions of cotton. Assistance from the hokimiat, like a school improvement, a bigger water system, or enhanced electrification, usually follows long and steady deliveries of cotton.

In Tashkent, the cotton assumes quite another value. The government sells the lint to textile mills in Switzerland, Italy, or elsewhere at a world market price usually exceeding $1,800 per ton, payable in hard currency. As a result of its longstanding "cottonization" program, newly independent Uzbekistan has entered the world economy as a major cotton producer, yielding 4 million tons annually. Only China and the United States consistently produce more. Very little of Uzbekistan's cotton profit filters down to the local level, and a severe gap in wealth has opened up between the trade-connected politicians and their merchants in Tashkent and everyone else in the country. Such a wide income gap is sadly typical of lesser-developed countries around the world.

CHAPTER

7

Regional Contrasts

U zbekistan is a country with one large city, Tashkent, a number of smaller cities, and hundreds of villages. The smaller cities predictably serve as commercial centers for nearby collective farm and resource-mining villages. Several of these cities were themselves imperial capitals only a century ago, and they occupy the richest oases in all of central Asia.

TASHKENT

Tashkent has been Uzbekistan's capital since 1930, and it was the Soviet Union's regional control center before 1991. Much of Central Asia is tectonically active, and Tashkent was destroyed by a series of earthquakes in 1966 and 1967. Much of the rebuilt city reflects the "gigantimania" that was a hallmark of Soviet architecture, made possible by the economics of cheap labor and building materials and free land. At the city center, big boxy government buildings punctuate

Pollution from a smokestack at a petrochemical plant lays a haze over the Tashkent landscape. Taskkent is a major urban center and has been the capital city since 1930.

vast open spaces and formal gardens. Immense fountains circulate huge volumes of evaporating water. Spacious high-rise hotels were built so foreign delegations could be shown Communism's "better way to advance the plight of 'backward' peoples." Boulevards were built extremely wide and straight and are only now approaching their traffic design capacities. Buses in Tashkent are clean and modern. Subway trains are fast and efficient, and the stations are elaborate.

Standard housing is the six- or nine-story apartment block assembled from prefabricated concrete slabs. Each unit houses hundreds of people, but they often have inadequate parking, so cars are commonly stuck into every nook and cranny. Lying at the upstream end of Uzbekistan, Tashkent is well watered and enjoys a healthy urban forest. Most Tashkenters are a walk or a bus ride away from one of the large outdoor food bazaars, with separate alleys for meat, vegetables, melons, or spices. Liquor, hardware, and toiletries are sold there as well. There is a festive mood in the bazaars, especially on weekends; visitors can enjoy an open-air meal of *shashlik* (shish-ka-bobs) or *plov* (a bowl of vegetables and lamb meat over rice) with hot tea.

In downtown Tashkent, there is a shopping street popularly called Broadway, which provides Uzbek crafts and Soviet-era souvenirs for tourists. Russian opera, Uzbek folkdancing and literary performances are offered in theaters at a cost that is a real bargain by Western standards. There are also a number of Western-style theme bars and restaurants in Tashkent, mostly in the hotels, that cater to visitors with hard currency. Russian food is frequently served in the hotels, as is vodka. The enterprising diner can also find a few Korean eateries, reflecting the fact that Koreans in the Soviet Far East were forcibly relocated here in the mid-twentieth century. Discos are dark and cramped drinking establishments flooded with the music that the privileged youth of Uzbekistan believe is popular in Europe and the United States. Very little conversation occurs here; these places are for dancing and smoking and looking. The world has come to Tashkent through the open door of television or, rather, the world as television depicts it. CNN and BBC (dubbed into Uzbek) are available, as is India's StarTV, with popular music videos from Asia and beyond, and hit shows (also dubbed) from Europe and the United States. Russian television programs are generally available, including old war movies, but the standard fare is Uzbek news, most of which features the daily accomplishments of President Karimov.

There is an old Tashkent of narrow, winding streets and compact adobe (mud brick) houses, but this is a small remnant that is overshadowed by modernized, Russified Tashkent. Ancient Tashkent was ruled by the khan of Kokand but was taken by the Russians in 1865 as a sort of preemptive strike against an anticipated attack on the city by the emir of Bukhara. The Russian capture of Tashkent is a classic example of intraregional rivalries opening the door to outside invasion. The Soviets industrialized Tashkent using hydroelectricity produced from the nearby Chirchik River. They developed a manufacturing base here, first for farm and cotton-picking machinery, then for armaments to help defend the Soviet Union in World War II, and finally for construction materials and light manufacturing for the rebuilding of Tashkent in the 1960s.

FERGANA VALLEY

East of Tashkent, after crossing dry foothills, a bus (they are inexpensive and run frequently) carries tourists and travelers into the fertile and productive Fergana Valley. The first stop on a counterclockwise tour around the valley is Kokand—essentially a farming city. There is little sign of Kokand's glorious past and the power that rivaled that of Bukhara. The khan's palace, from which he ruled the entire valley and lands all the way to the Aral Sea shore, stands downtown next to an amusement park. A handful of mosques bear witness to Kokand's traditional religious significance dating back to the sixteenth century. Farms, located 20 miles (30 kilometers) east or west and 13 miles (20 kilometers) north or south from central Kokand, produce cotton, rice, grapes, and fruits. The local economy relies mainly on the production of fertilizers, chemicals, farm machinery, and, of course, cotton.

Farther to the east are the cities of Farghona and Margilan. Farghona is the administrative center of the valley and was built by the Russians according to a modern grid layout. Wide streets and an active central business district contain offices of the Russian General Skobolev, who annexed Central Asia to the Russian Empire in the 1860s. Farghona is an industrial city in the heart of farming country. Supported by nearby hydroelectric generation, factory workers weave textiles, make glass, and power light manufacturing. There is a food-processing industry, relatively rare in Uzbekistan, and there are also more than two dozen heavy industrial complexes producing fertilizer

The Fergana Valley is a major agricultural area and produces many products, such as onions, cotton, rice, grapes, and other fruits.

and cement and refining petrochemicals. Despite the presence of these heavier industries, Farghona is remarkably clean and a very pleasant place. With its dense tree cover, running streams, and a spectacular view of the Alay Mountains to the south, Farghona was a popular tourist destination in the Soviet era. Nearby Margilan is hundreds of years older than Farghona; it remains thoroughly agricultural and is a center for the collection and weaving of silk.

At the northeastern corner of the valley is Andijon, another industrial city surrounded by a sea of irrigated cotton. It was a major stop on the caravan route between the Persian and Chinese empires and was seized by Russia in 1876. Andijon's biggest industry is cotton textile manufacturing, and hundreds of tons of thread are shipped to Russian and European customers every month. The Fergana Valley is underlain by significant oil and gas reserves, and Andijon has a new modern underground natural gas storage facility. The South Korean automaker Daewoo has recently opened an assembly plant near Andijon with a 1.86-mile-long (3-kilometer) conveyor line.

Circling back nearly 50 miles (80 kilometers) west of Andijon is Namangan, an ancient city seemingly filled with children. Since independence, the government of Uzbekistan has been rushing to expand economic opportunities in the Fergana Valley, and Namangan demonstrates why. There are now more than 2 million people around Namangan, with only about 300,000 of them living inside the city. There are also very few jobs in the area. Long hot summers aggravate youthful impatience, and the observer can understand why the Russians might have been so ready to disengage from Central Asia when the USSR disintegrated. In May 1989, for instance, a rude exchange over the quality of fruit in a bazaar ignited an ethnic war that raged for weeks, spread to neighboring towns, and left 112 people dead.

Since independence, many underemployed young men of Namangan have been occupying themselves with studying the Koran and attending politically charged lectures at any number of new mosques. A strict interpretation of Sunni Islam espoused by the Wahabis of Saudi Arabia has become popular here and is gaining favor with some students in Tashkent as well. They study the Arabic alphabet, rather than the business-oriented Latin alphabet used in the capitalist West. Some have joined local militias in order to enforce a higher moral order, interrupting crimes and turning in criminals to the police. Some work sporadically for any one of several hundred formerly state-owned enterprises that are now officially privatized. In truth, these privatized businesses have simply lost their price supports and guaranteed markets. All around the area, however (and this is true over much of the Fergana Valley), cotton is still king and the main employer. Namangan resembles a large farm labor camp.

CITIES OF THE GOLADNAYA STEPPE

Dropping out of the Fergana Valley on the way to Samarkand, the traveler crosses a sloping plain under an unbroken sky and passes a monotonous and seemingly endless chain of cotton fields. This is the Goladnaya (Hungry) Steppe, a 2.2-million-acre (one-million-hectare) tract whose transformation from desert waste to productive farmland was one of a dozen such projects begun in the tsarist era and greatly expanded by the Soviets. Its name is deceptive in that its primary contribution to "hunger" is fibrous cotton for export. It is, however, a hungry place for water from the Syr Darya, and the basin's irrigation network now receives more water than the Syr delivers to the Aral Sea.

At the southern end of the Goladnaya Steppe is the town of Jizzakh (population 120,000). Jizzakh was an ancient Silk Road town that guarded a pass between mountains on the east and hills on the west and was an important gateway to Samarkand. Today, the city serves as a significant cotton collection and ginning station. Finally, it is the burial site of the old Communist Party boss Sharaf Rashidov. For years, Rashidov swindled Russians by diverting cotton payments to his favorite clan subordinates, steadily raising those payments by collecting inflated sums supported by falsified production figures. Eventually, the scheme was exposed by accountants in Moscow, and Rashidov's reign ended with what was reported as a "heart attack" in 1983. He was maligned in death and buried in Jizzakh without fanfare. Being condemned by Moscow, however, was a badge of honor in Jizzakh, and President Karimov later raised his own local popularity when he rehabilitated Rashidov's reputation with a portrait, a street name, a plaque for his birth place, and a monument for his gravesite.

MAGNIFICENT SAMARKAND

Sixty miles (100 kilometers) farther southward is Samarkand (Samarqand), which rises from the banks of the Zeravshan River. The city is the administrative center of its own province of

These students at a school in Samarkand illustrate a modern, working city with a fabled past. One of the great cities of the world, Samarkand was centrally located on the Silk Road. It has been inhabited for over 12,000 years.

2.4 million people, and Samarkand itself is home to half a million. Acknowledged as one of the greatest cities in the world, Samarkand is situated on a fertile grassy steppe with mountain streams tumbling through. It was centrally located on the Silk Road—connecting westward to Bukhara and to Arabia far beyond, southward with Persia (Iran), and eastward to China and Mongolia. People have lived here for at least 12,000 years— more than 7,000 years before Egyptians built the great pyramids. Buried beneath the 2,500- to 3,000-year-old Samarkand is the old mud city of Marakanda, which is 3,000 years older than Samarkand. Alexander the Great loved Marakanda, parts of which can be visited today, and its excavation will continue for generations to come. The best-known sites in the area are considerably newer and were built for the man who made Samarkand his own, Timur (Tamerlane). The huge *madrassas* (religious schools), imposing tombs, magnificent mosques (one of which was the world's largest building), holy Muslim sites, and Timur's own family mausoleum together are the legendary Samarkand, a city virtually unknown to the Western world until the 1870s.

When the Chinese sealed their borders in the fifteenth century and Europeans took to the sea, traffic on the Silk Road thinned. Samarkand faded from glory and eventually fell under the control of Bukhara until Russia occupied the region in 1868. The Russians ignored its history and concentrated on acquiring its cotton. The railroad came in 1888, and not much else happened until 1924, when Samarkand was briefly named capital of the new Uzbek Soviet Socialist Republic. Through the Soviet era, Samarkand collected cotton, silk, and tea. It has been home to tanneries, canneries, light manufacturing, and major universities. Samarkand today is very much a working city, but its mystique is deeply rooted and visitors still stand in awe before its great temples. In 1941, more than 500 years after his death, Soviet archeologists finally unsealed Timur's tomb. Among their findings was Timur's warning of dire consequences for anyone who disturbed his resting place. Almost simultaneously, Nazi Germany invaded the Soviet Union.

BUKHARA

Downstream along the Zeravshan River lies the fascinating city of Bukhara (Buxoro). In the center of Bukhara is an intact city dating to the time of Genghis Khan. The city remained autonomous longer than any other city in central Asia (until 1924). The emir's country palace is still a splendid example of excess, and his great citadel, called the Ark, still lords over the city center. The later khans of Bukhara called themselves emirs, but the early kingdom distinguished itself with its size. At its

The center of Bukhara is an intact city dating to the time of Genghis Khan. This old trading house has a 500-year-old canal threading beneath its structures.

peak in the late 1500s, Bukhara controlled the Fergana Valley, Tashkent, today's northern Afghanistan, and most of the length of the Oxus River—now called the Amu. Four hundred years earlier, it was one of Islam's great capital cities.

Bukhara once boasted more than 300 mosques, and it still has a number of splendid and very well attended holy sites. Just as Samarkand had Ulug Beg, one of the greatest of all astronomers, Bukhara was home to Avicenna, the father of modern medicine. The darker side of Bukhara's story involves the meanness of its emirs. They were noted for their dungeons, slavery, and brutal executions at the same time they indulged in self-adornment and notorious sexual escapades. Bukhara is special, however, because of its earlier history of learning and reverence. The city's past is especially useful to the government's program of building an Uzbekistani identity. In 1997, Bukhara celebrated 2,500 years of existence. After decades of neglect, however, Bukhara's mosques and tombs are deteriorating, quite beyond the government's budget for restoration. Dedicated artisans patiently replaster and reglaze, but their efforts pale before the magnitude of the task. Still, Bukharans are a patient people; they know that everything takes time.

By 1920, Bukhara was surrounded by Soviet Turkistan and was failing economically. The emir was deposed that year, and Bukhara was ceded to Uzbekistan in 1924. The atheist Communists faced a dilemma in gaining responsibility for the holy city of Bukhara, and they decided to let it die. The city was saved by water.

Bukhara is on the Zeravshan Delta and is one of the few areas of Ukzbekistan with watered alluvial lands (land with sediment deposited by running water). During the early years of the Soviet era, when the city's population fell by half, the area's collective farm villages grew. Gradually, the city did what cities do: It focused on specialists and services that reversed its deterioration. With the help of a new water supply (Amu diversions) in the 1960s, Bukhara has crawled back to support a quarter-million people, only 20 percent fewer than a millennium ago.

Bukharans shop in the city's bazaars. There are a few department stores, like the semistocked hardware and dry goods store. Bukhara is fairly remote, so whatever halting progress is seen in irrigation facilities, private leasing of land, or public transportation in Tashkent, is barely perceptible here. The buses are typically 1970s-vintage Ikarus models, and they are a compliment to Hungarian engineering if not pollution control. The favorite activity here is sitting or lying in the *chaikhona* (tea house) with friends. People walk a great deal, tend their gardens, and enjoy themselves. A busy American could do well to slow down in Bukhara.

Patching a roof in Bukhara involves re-mudding it by hand.

KHIVA

Pushing westward and approaching the Amu Delta is the living museum city of Khiva. Its current population is barely 40,000, but from 1592 to 1920, it was the seat of Khivan khans. It was an essential *caravansary* (rest stop) on the Silk Road and ran a slave-based economy. Time and again, entire Russian armies perished in failed attempts to conquer the city. Khiva is also sort of a living fantasy. Its origins are said to date back to Shem, one of Noah's sons, but no one is sure if this is so. Its medieval buildings are remarkably preserved but devoid of life. Although Bukhara's great outer wall is mostly gone, Khiva's wall remains intact. In fact, so much of Khiva has been rebuilt that tourists sometimes feel they are roaming through a 500-year old theme park.

Khiva's modern neighbor, and a real working city, is Urganch. It is as plain as Khiva is ornate. A gritty labor town on

A camel ride in Khiva recalls the days when the city was a *caravansary,* or rest stop, on the Silk Road.

an important rail line to Moscow, it has a minor cotton and food-processing center and is home to 120,000 people.

CITIES OF THE SOUTH

In Uzbekistan's southernmost Kaska Darya and Surkan Darya provinces are the towns of Shakrisabz, Karshi (Qarshi), and Termez. Shakrisabz, which occupies its own small valley, is the birthplace of Timur and the burial site of Timurid kings, including two of Timur's sons. A burial place dug for Timur himself remains open and empty. Shakrisabz was also the site of one of Timur's greatest palaces, although the building is now gone. Its entranceway was 150 feet tall. The town of 60,000 is surrounded by vineyards and fruit trees and is popular with collectors of folk-art embroidery. Not far downslope is the

Karshi Steppe and an immense cotton-growing region, complete with an elaborate irrigation network augmented by water imported from the Amu. The city of Karshi was once an important trading center between Samarkand and Bukhara and points south; it was also another of Timur's favorite residences. Now it is home to 200,000 people and is the regional processing center for cotton, grain, and tobacco harvests. Termez lies on the ancient frontier of Zoroastrian cities (the people of the first religion), Buddhist migrations, and Persian, Greek, Arab, and Mongol conquests. Today, the city is Uzbekistan's gateway to Afghanistan.

REGIONAL DIVISIONS

Uzbekistan's subregions and urban centers have assumed new and renewed significance since the 1990s. The Uzbek economy has tightened since independence, and the average citizen's lifestyle has changed accordingly. Among the consequences of this belt-tightening are that people travel less than they did during the Soviet era and are more concerned with their own well being, and less concerned with consequences affecting others.

If we remember that clean water is necessary for quality living, that Uzbekistan is dry in the west and less dry in the east, and that the country generally slopes downward from east to west, we can see a pecking order emerge. Easterners take water at will and dump their wastes back into the streams with less and less regard for the effects of a shrunken and tainted water supply on later users. Ultimately, the downstream water drinkers and irrigators are left with deteriorating water quality, compromised health, shrinking economies, and damaged soils. At the end of the Amu, for instance, the river laces its putrid soup through the shrinking wetlands of Karakalpakistan. Backtracking upstream, casual conversations confirm what the government ignores—that residents of the tailwater zones are victimized by upstream and midstream consumers and wasters and practically no one cares.

It is ironic that with the rise of free speech in the final years of the Soviet Union, the government of the Uzbek SSR expressed outrage over Moscow's long exploitation of local farmlands and over an uncaring attitude for the downstream victims of that exploitation. Early environmental protests in Uzbekistan even energized a nationalist movement. Those attracted to this movement resented the soil destruction, health alerts, and ruin of the Aral Sea and considered these an assault on Uzbekistan. More than a decade after independence from the USSR, however, the same hated policies continue. Only the protests are gone. Karakalpaks, of course, complain to whoever will listen, and there is talk of secession from Uzbekistan, but few Uzbekistanis seem to care.

UZBEKISTAN AND ITS NEIGHBORS

Just as Uzbekistan has internal subregional contrasts and conflicts, the country is now at the center of a complicated greater region, and this region is changing quickly. As one of five Soviet central Asian republics, the Uzbek Soviet Socialist Republic was an internal unit of the USSR. Outside ties with Uzbekistan were restricted because the USSR was a closed and internally integrated empire. Now that the imperial barrier is lifted, real foreign relations are developing between Uzbekistan and its neighbors.

Watchers of central Asia are now observing a network of relations that did not exist before and was not widely anticipated even after independence. That network of relations is between the former Soviet central Asian republics, all of which are now independent countries and none of which has a mature economy, free democracy, or unified society. Those republics are (clockwise) Kazakhstan, Kyrgyzstan, Tajikistan, and Turkmenistan. In the middle is Uzbekistan. This pivotal position in a reforming region makes Uzbekistan a very important place, especially when one considers the following:

A boy drives his sheep along the frontier that separates Afghanistan from Uzbekistan. Now that the Soviet Union is no more, foreign relations are developing between Uzbekistan and its neighbors.

- Uzbekistan has more people than all of the surrounding republics combined.

- Uzbekistan contains many important and historic urban and cultural centers in central Asia, including Bukhara, Khiva, Kokand, Samarkand, Marakanda, and Tashkent, the tsarist and Soviet capital of Turkistan.

- Uzbekistan commands most of the fertile Fargana Valley, holds the region's widest expanse of productive steppelands, and dominates the Aral Sea area.

- There are large Uzbek minority populations in all of the regional countries: 420,000 (2.5 percent of the total population) in Kazakhstan, 2.4 million (8 percent) in Afghanistan, 470,000 (10 percent) in Turkmenistan, 620,000 (13 percent) in Kyrgyzstan, and 1.7 million in Tajikistan (25 percent).

- Uzbekistan has the largest and most potent military force in Central Asia.

- Political instability in Uzbekistan would almost surely spill over into neighboring countries.

- The government of Uzbekistan has raised the idea of Turkistan. No other regional government has done this. From its influence and central position, it is clear that Uzbekistan could gain regional power from the resurrection of a panregional, secular (nonreligious) governing structure.

Observers of the region also recognize that there was no rivalry among Soviet Central-Asian republics prior to 1991. Political life was simpler then. Ethnic and clan divisions paled in comparison to the general sense of opposition that everyone felt toward Moscow. Soviet oppression was even a unifying force among central Asians. Prejudice existed but was almost forgotten. Now it has returned, with disputes centering on water rights more than on any other single issue.

Such disputes include Uzbek demands that the government of Tajikistan fully water the Uzbek village of Kolkhozabad, which is *inside* Tajikistan, and that the Tajiks stop chemical dumping into the Vakhsh River (a main tributary of the Amu). Turkmenistan is demanding greater freshwater diversions from Uzbekistan into the Kara Kum Canal. At the same time, however, Uzbek settlers and fighters in Afghanistan occupy the headwaters of Turkmenistan's only two natural rivers, the Tejen and Murgab, so the Turkmen demand is weakened somewhat.

Kyrgyzstan demands that Uzbekistan help maintain the Kyrgyz reservoir system because it was built to provide Uzbek farms with timely irrigation. The Uzbeks counter with complaints about irradiated runoff from a Kyrgyz uranium mine, with demands for additional Fergana Valley lands, and with threats to cut off natural gas deliveries.

In a curious development, peace in Afghanistan could actually harm Uzbekistan. Economic development in northern Afghanistan would result in greater withdrawals of Kokcha and Konduz waters, and these rivers both flow into the Amu Darya. Unfortunately for thirsty midstream and downstream Uzbekistan, northern Afghanistan has fertile soils and rests on significant natural gas deposits. Northern Afghanistan, therefore, can be expected to develop quickly under peaceful and stable conditions. Still, it would be difficult to argue that Afghan chaos is in Uzbekistan's best interest. In contrast, cautious stewardship of Central Asia's fresh water—everywhere along the line—is.

CHAPTER

8

Uzbekistan
Looks Ahead

U
zbekistan's future began with independence in the spring of 1991. At that time, the country joined the club of sovereign nations and took stock of its assets and liabilities. Like most new countries, it has emerged onto the world stage bearing a set of difficult challenges. These challenges are diverse but interconnected. Solving any one of them could lead to solving others. Failing to solve them could lead Uzbekistan into chaos.

Uzbekistan's leaders must find a way to stop or to economically provide for an explosive population growth. They must continue their efforts to unify the people of the country by cultivating state nationalism. They must find ways to solve regional disputes over water and eliminate environmentally damaging practices. They must also gain access to the world trading community.

From the developed Western world, observers have been able to watch Uzbekistan's growing pains from a detached perspective, but

This flock of children on a street in Bukhara is typical of this country of colorful people in a dynamic place and time in the world.

this detachment is a quickly evaporating luxury. If modern world events teach us anything, it is that globalization narrows the distances between far-flung lands. This is especially obvious in recent events that have demonstrated new and unstable connections between the United States and central Asia. In the aftermath of terrorist bombings against the United States on September 11, 2001, the U.S. military has negotiated basing privileges at the Khanabad Air Base near Karshi. From this position, the United States has had a staging area for its war to overthrow the Taliban regime in Afghanistan and in its search for al-Qaeda fighters throughout the region. Uzbekistan is suddenly attracting world attention to a degree not seen since the era of the Great Silk Road.

The United States has injected its military presence into Uzbekistan against a backdrop of growing youthful frustrations with a slow economy and an undercurrent of rising Islamic militancy. American forces are a very foreign transplant onto the Karshi Steppe, and the United States' imprint will inevitably be associated with policies of the government of Uzbekistan. Over the long term, Uzbekistan is scheduled to receive $8 billion dollars for this basing arrangement—a huge sum of money for a state with a $4 billion total federal budget in 2002.

Observers might also conclude that Uzbekistan is in a good position. It has a comprehensive program (and perhaps even enough time) to nurture state nationalism. It has enlisted international attention and money with its rich energy base and sensitive strategic position. Potential predator-states have turned out to be generally reserved and respectful of Uzbekistani self-determination. The greater region of middle and southern Asia, after a long and serious escalation of tensions, may now be moving toward peace and stability.

Market reforms certainly could stimulate the economy and raise environmental awareness. With the country's vast energy and other mineral deposits, however, it will be difficult, and perhaps even destabilizing, for the leadership to release its hold on national asset flows. Even without capitalism shock therapy, the government of Uzbekistan may be able to retune the economy in meaningful ways. With Uzbekistan's potential to feed growing domestic and regional populations, for example, even incremental improvements in food processing, packaging, and transportation could stimulate a major employer industry and turn the country into a serious product exporter.

Uzbekistan is a rich country of colorful people in a dynamic part of the world. It also presents important opportunities for the West, especially to those countries who have an interest in cultivating friendly relations with young ambitious Muslim peoples and learning about great cultures and our place among them. The West also stands to gain in economic and environmental terms. By working with an important oil and gas producer, Western nations have the opportunity to expand their markets for technology and promote economic prosperity in a volatile part of the world. They can also monitor and assist environmental restoration on a global scale.

Despite its challenges, Uzbekistan is wealthy in natural and human resources. Visitors are welcome and well treated. The country has been closed to the outside world for a very long time, so outsiders have an excellent opportunity to make a positive and lasting first impression. Uzbekistan is also a place where visitors can reflect on nature, on purpose, and on humanity. No one who visits Uzbekistan can remain unmoved.

Fact at a Glance

Country Name	Uzbekiston Respublikasi (Republic of Uzbekistan)
Common Name	Uzbekistan
Former Name	Uzbek Soviet Socialist Republic
Capital	Tashkent
Country Flag	Commissioned November 18, 1991, at the eighth session of the Supreme Soviet of Uzbekistan. It has three equal horizontal bands of green at the bottom (representing nature), white in the middle (representing purity of purpose), and blue on the top (sky blue—Emir Timur's flag was this color). The horizontal bands are separated by ribbons of red (life force). In the upper left quadrant is a large white crescent moon (Peaceful Islam) and 12 white stars (12 hokimiats).
State Seal	Commissioned July 2, 1992. At the center is the Humo bird with wings spread (happiness and freedom) anchored to Uzbekistan. The father of Uzbek literature, Alisher Navoi, called the Humo the greatest living creature. The rising sun represents everything good; the images of desert and steppe represent the republic's dominant features. On the top is a crescent moon and star. The sheaf of wheat and bundle of cotton (bountiful land) are held together by strips of the flag (solidarity of the people).
Membership in International Organizations	Asian Development Bank, Customs Cooperation Council, Commonwealth of Independent States, Euro-Atlantic Partnership Council, European Bank for Reconstruction & Development, Economic Commission for Europe, Economic Cooperation Organization, Food & Agricultural Organization, International Atomic Energy Agency, International Bank for Reconstruction & Development, International Civil Aviation Organization, International Committee for Radionuclide Metrology, International Federation of Red Cross and Red Crescent Societies, International Labor Organization, International Monetary Fund, Interpol, International Olympic Committee, International Organization for

Standardization, International Telecommunication Union, Non-Aligned Movement, Organization of the Islamic Conference, Organization for the Prohibition of Chemical Weapons, Organization for Security and Cooperation in Europe, Partnership for Peace (with NATO), United Nations, UN Conference on Trade & Development, UN Economic Commission for Europe, UN Educational Scientific & Cultural Organization, UN Economic & Social Commission for Asia and the Pacific, UN Industrial Development Organization, Universal Postal Union, World Bank, World Federation of Trade Unions, World Health Organization, World Intellectual Property Organization, World Meteorological Organization, World Tourism Organization, World Trade Organization (observer status).

Independence Day	August 31, 1991 (from Soviet Union).

Physical Geography

Total Area	173,591 square miles (449,601 square kilometers); slightly larger than California or larger than the United Kingdom, Belgium, Denmark, Switzerland, and Austria combined. The distance west to east is 885 miles (1,425 kilometers) and from north to south, 578 miles (930 kilometers).
Latitude/Longitude	37–46 degrees North, 56–73 degrees East.
Border Countries	Kazakhstan, 1,377-mile (2,203-kilometer) border; Kyrgyzstan, 687-mile (1,099-kilometer) border; Tajikistan, 726-mile (1,161-kilometer) border; Afghanistan, 86-mile (137-kilometer) border; Turkmenistan, 1,013-mile (1,621-kilometer) border.
Climate	Mostly midlatitude desert and steppe, with long hot summers and moderately cold winters; semiarid grassland in east.

People

Population	25,600,000 (August 2002 estimate).
Population Growth Rate	1.7 percent (2002 estimate); births (26 per 1,000 population) minus deaths (8 per 1,000 population).

Fact at a Glance

Life Expectancy at Birth Total population: 63.9 years; female: 67.6 years; male: 60.4 years.

Total Fertility Rate 3.03 children born per woman (2002 estimate).

Literacy 97 percent (age 15 years and older can read and write); female: 96 percent; male: 98 percent.

Ethnic Groups Uzbek, 80 percent; Tajik, 5 percent; Kazakh, 4 percent; Karakalpak, 4 percent; Russian, 4 percent.

Religions Muslim, 88 percent (mostly Sunni); Eastern Orthodox, 9 percent; other, 3 percent.

Government

Type of Government Republic with strong central government. Strong executive branch with executive power concentrated in the presidency and weaker unicameral legislature and judiciary—itself led by a Supreme Court whose members are nominated by the president and confirmed by legislature.

Executive Leadership President Islom Abduganievich Karimov (elected March 24, 1990, by the Supreme Soviet).

Prime Minister Otkir Sultonov (appointed December 21, 1995).

Cabinet of Ministers Appointed by the president and approved by legislature.

Administrative Arrangement Uzbekistan is subdivided into 12 hokimiats (regions) and one autonomous republic (Karakalpakistan).

Economy

Cities over 250,000 in population Tashkent (capital), Samarkand, Andijon, Namangan, Bukhara

Cities over 100,000 13 total

GDP $60 billion (2000 estimate).

GDP/Purchasing Power Parity $65 billion (2001 estimate).

GDP per capita $2,344

GDP per capita/PPP $2,500

GDP Growth Rate 3 percent (2001 estimate).

GDP by Sector	Agriculture, 33 percent; industry, 24 percent; services, 43 percent (2000 estimate).
Main Products	Cotton, silk vegetables, fruits, natural gas, oil, gold, copper, machinery, chemicals.
State Budget	Revenues: $4 billion; expenditures: $4.1 billion (1999 estimate).
Exports	$2.8 billion f.o.b. (2001 estimate): cotton, 41.5 percent; gold, 9.5 percent; energy products, 9.5 percent; mineral fertilizers, ferrous metals, textiles, food products, automobiles (1998 estimate).
Export Partners	Russia, 16 percent; Switzerland, 9 percent; United Kingdom, 8 percent; Ukraine, 4.5 percent; South Korea, 3.5 percent; Kazakhstan 3 percent (2000).
Imports	$2.5 billion f.o.b. (2001 estimate): machinery and equipment, 50 percent; foodstuffs, 16.5 percent; chemicals, metals (1998 estimate).
Import Partners	Russia, 16 percent; South Korea, 10 percent; United States, 8.7 percent; Germany, 9 percent; Kazakhstan, 7.5 percent; Ukraine, 6 percent (2002).
Currency	1 *sum* = 100 *tiyin*.
Exchange Rate	970 sum per U.S. dollar (May 2003).
Labor force	12 million.
Occupations by Sector	Agriculture, 45 percent; industry, 20 percent; services, 35 percent.

History at a Glance

330 B.C.	Alexander the Great invaded from the south and west, stayed long enough to take a wife, and exited to the south and east.
100 B.C. – A.D. 300	Persians ruled the territories of modern-day Uzbekistan.
710	Arab Muslim invaders reached Bukhara, which became an important city in the Islamic world during the Crusades (late eleventh, twelfth, and thirteenth centuries).
980–1037	Avicenna, Arabic philosopher and physician, wrote, taught, and invented in Bukhara.
1072–1092	Seljukid leader Melik Shah, based in the region that is today's Uzbekistan, led the mightiest empire in southwest Asia.
1167–1227	Genghis Khan (Khan Chingis), and his sons after him, ruled the world's largest land empire.
1370–1405	Timur (Tamerlane) built a great and fearsome empire from his seat of power at Samarkand.
1497	Vasco de Gama began his voyage around Africa from Europe. The Great Silk Road, which moved people, goods, and ideas across Middle Asia, began to decline in importance.
1717	Russia's first march on Khiva ended in failure; several more failures followed.
1865–1881	Russia conquered important central Asian power bases (Tashkent, Samarkand, Khiva, and Kokand) and surrounded Bukhara.
1917	The Russian tsarist empire fell, and the inhabitants of today's Uzbekistan tried to free themselves from Russian control.
1924	While the people were still fighting the new Soviet Army for their freedom, the USSR declared the formation of an Uzbek Soviet Socialist Republic.
1928–1933	Soviet authorities shut down most mosques in Uzbekistan.
1930s	Soviet authorities purged Uzbek literature of authenticity.
1937	Soviet authorities accused Uzbek leaders of insufficient devotion to the Communist Party; most were purged.

1959	Sharaf Rashidov is named first secretary of the Uzbek Communist Party.
1983	Sharaf Rashidov and his leadership are accused of corruption and purged.
1991	September 1, Uzbekistan declares independence from the Soviet Union.

Further Reading

Akiner, Shireen. *Islamic Peoples of the Soviet Union.* London: KPI, 1986.

Alexeiv, Alex. *Gorbachev's Muslim Dilemma.* Santa Monica, CA: Rand Corp., 1987.

Alworth, Edward. *The Modern Uzbeks: From the Fourteenth Century to the Present.* Stanford, CA: Stanford Press, 1990.

Critchlow, James. *Nationalism in Uzbekistan: A Soviet Republic's Road to Sovereignty.* Boulder, CO: Westview Press, 1991.

Dienes, Leslie. *Soviet Asia: Economic Development and National Policy Choices.* Boulder, CO: Westview Press, 1987.

Ferdinand, Peter, ed. *The New States of Central Asia and Their Neighbors.* New York: Council on Foreign Relations, 1994.

Feshbach and Friendly, Jr., "Cradle to Grave." *Ecocide in the USSR: Health and Nature Under Siege.* New York: Basic Books. 1992.

Fierman, William. *Soviet Central Asia: The Failed Transformation.* Boulder, CO: Westview Press, 1991.

Gleason, Gregory. "Uzbekistan: From Statehood to Nationhood?" In *Nations and Politics in the Soviet Successor States*, ed., Ian Bremmer and Ray Taras, pp. 331–360. Cambridge, MA: Cambridge University Press, 1993.

Helsinki Watch. *Human Rights in Uzbekistan.* Human Rights Watch, 1993.

Hopkirk, Peter. *The Great Game: The Struggle for Empire in Central Asia.* New York: Kodansha International, 1994.

Kaiser, Robert. "Ethnoterritorial Conflict in the former-Soviet Union: Summary and Discussion," The Challenges of Ethnic Conflict to National and International Order in the 1990s: Geographic Perspectives. CIA, RTT95–10039 October 1995, p. 72.

Karimov, Islom Abduganievich. *Uzbekistan on the Threshold of the Twenty-first Century: Challenges to Stability and Progress.* New York: Palgrave Macmillan, 1998.

Liebowitz, Ronald D. "Spatial Inequality Under Gorbachev." In *The Soviet Union: A New Regional Geography*, ed. Michael Bradshaw, p. 23. New York: Bellhaven Press, 1991.

Lubin, Nancy. *Calming The Ferghana Valley: Development and Dialogue in the Heart of Central Asia.* New York: Council on Foreign Relations, Century Foundation, Center for Preventive Action.

Malcomson, Scott. *Borderlands: Nation and Empire*. London: Faber & Faber, 1994.

Magowan, Robin. *Fabled Cities of Central Asia: Samarkand, Bukhara, Khiva*. New York: Abbeville Press, 1990.

Micklin, Philip P., and William D. Williams, eds. *The Aral Sea Basin*. New York: Springer-Verlag, 1996.

Radio Free Europe/Radio Liberty: Central Asia Report. newsline3-subscribe

Roi, Yaacov. *The USSR and the Muslim World*. London: George Allen & Unwin, 1984.

Smith, David R. "Change and Variability in Climate and Ecosystem Decline in Aral Sea Basin Deltas." *Post-Soviet Geography*, March 1994, pp.142–165.

Thubron, Colin. *The Lost Heart of Asia*. New York: HarperCollins, 1994.

Thurman, Michael. "Leaders of the Communist Party of Uzbekistan in Historical Retrospect: The Class of '38." *Central Asia Monitor*, 6, 1995.

Websites

Central Intelligence Agency. *World Factbook*. Washington, DC *www.cia.gov/cia/publications/factbook/geos/ic.html*.

U.S. Department of State. Background Notes. *http://www.state.gov/r/pa/ei/bgn/3396.htm*.

Index

Abdulla Khan, 20
Afghanistan, 10, 27, 51, 56, 68, 83, 87, 90, 91, 93
agriculture, 10, 12, 14, 16, 19-25, 32, 33, 34, 36, 40, 46, 54-55, 58-59, 61, 71, 73, 77, 78, 87-89.
    See also cotton/cottonization
aircraft, 56
Alay Mountains, 15, 78
Alexander II, 29
Alexander the Great, 26, 27, 81
allegiance, 36-43, 46-53, 83-84, 92, 94
alphabet, 35, 39, 79
al-Qaeda, 93
Amu Darya, 10, 16, 18-19, 21, 24, 68, 83, 87, 91
Amu Darya Delta, 21, 61
Amu-Bakhara Canal, 68
Anatolian Peninsula, 27
Andijon, 34, 52
animal husbandry, 21
animal life, 21
Arabic alphabet, 39, 79
Arabic language, 42
Aral Drainage Basin, 23, 69
Aral Kum (Aral Desert), 22, 23-24
Aral Sea, 10, 15, 17-25, 67, 68, 70, 80, 88, 89
Aral Sea Basin, 16
area, 10
Ark, 82
army, 90
Ashgabat, Turkmenistan, 12
astronomy, 26, 83
authoritarianism, 10-11
automobiles, 56, 59, 60, 75, 79
Avicenna, 83

Baghdad, 27
bartering, 58-59
bazaars, 58-59, 60, 75-76, 84
birds, 21
black market, 60, 65
Bolshevik Revolution, 30
borders, 10, 12, 15, 16, 46, 51, 68, 87
building materials industry, 56
Bukhara (Buxoro), 20, 26, 28, 30, 31, 34, 36, 40, 47, 52, 61, 68, 76, 77, 82-84, 89
Butofos, 23

canals, 67-68
capital city. *See* Tashkent
capitalism, 10
caravansary (rest stop), 85
chaikhona (tea house), 84
Chirchik River, 77
cities, 12, 26, 34, 60, 74-87.
    See also Tashkent
civil war, 62
clans, 36-37, 39-40, 44, 47, 52, 63, 65
climate/weather, 12, 14-16, 19, 21, 23, 24
collective farm. *See kolkhoz*
colonialism, 10
communication, 59, 60, 76
Communist Party, 33, 37, 39, 45, 52, 60, 80
consumer goods, 58-59, 60
copper, 56
corruption, 10
cotton scandals, 65, 80
cotton/cottonization, 19, 20, 21, 23, 24, 29, 31, 35, 40, 46, 54, 58, 60, 61-71, 73, 77-80, 82, 86-88
Crusaders, 26

culture, 10, 11, 27, 39, 40-43, 63, 76, 83
currency, 60
Cyrillic alphabet, 35, 39

Daewoo, 79
Dargom canal system, 20
Dark Ages, 27-28
dekan (peasant farmworker), 58-59, 62
Delhi, 27, 48-49
democracy, 10
deputy prime ministers, 44
deserts, 10, 14
dress, 40
dust storms, 23-24

earthquakes, 12, 21, 31, 33
ecology lottery, 46
economy, 10, 11, 14, 20, 21, 24-25, 32, 33, 35-36, 47, 51, 54-71, 73, 87, 94. *See also* agriculture
education, 33, 34-36, 39, 42, 48-50, 56, 60, 82
electricity, 33, 60
Emir Timur Museum, 50
Emir Timur Square, 49-50
employment, 33
energy resources, 10, 14, 55, 56, 77, 79, 91, 94, 95
environmental concerns, 10, 17-25, 36, 46, 67, 71, 87-88, 90-91, 92, 94, 95
Eurasia, 10, 14
Europe, 10
exotic surface waters, 16
exports, 60, 63, 73, 94

family, 33, 37, 40-41, 44
Farghona, 34, 77

Fergana Valley, 12, 19, 24, 28, 31, 34, 42, 52, 61, 67, 77-79, 83, 89, 91
fertility rate, 32
fishing industry, 20, 21, 32
Five-year Plans, 62
food, 40, 60, 61, 62, 63, 75-76
food-processing industry, 77, 86, 94
foreign investment, 60
foreign policy, 10, 56-57, 88-91, 93-95
forests, 32, 75
fruits, 19, 40, 54-55, 77
future, 92-95

gardens, 58-59
Genghis Khan (Khan Chingis), 27, 48, 82
Germans, 33
glaciers, 16, 23
globalization, 92-93
Goek Tepe, 29
Goladnaya (Hungry) Steppe, 61, 80
gold, 10, 55-56
government, 10-11, 33-34, 42-43, 44-53, 63
grains, 19, 54
grapes, 77
Great Britain, Russia *versus*, 29, 31, 57
Great Fergana Canal, 20, 67
Great Game, 29, 31, 57
Great Silk Road. *See* Silk Road
Green Revolution, 64

hajj (pilgrimage), 42, 51
health concerns, 23, 24, 33, 63, 67, 87, 88
higher education, 35-36, 56, 82

Index

historiography, 39, 48-50

history, 10, 20, 26-31, 35, 39,
   61, 76, 81

hokim (provincial governor), 44,
   52

hokimiats (provincial
   governments), 44, 73

holidays, 41

housing, 33, 60, 75, 76

hydroelectricity, 77

independence, 31, 34, 45, 46-47,
   56, 92

India
   and Great Britain *versus*
      Russia, 29, 31, 57
   rail-highway pipeline corridor
      to, 56
   and Timur, 48-49

Indian Ocean, 56

Indo-Europeans, 26

Indo-Gangetic Plain, 27

Internet, 36

Iran, 57

irrigation, 16, 20, 24-25, 33,
   58, 62, 66, 67-70, 73, 80, 87,
   90-91

Islam, 10, 11
   and agriculture, 61
   arrival of in Bukara, 26
   and fall of Soviet Union,
      41-43
   and Mongols, 27, 29
   and mosques, 37, 42, 52, 77,
      79, 82, 83
   political, 51-52, 79
   and Russians, 34
   and Soviet Union, 30, 37-38,
      40
   and Sufism, 50-51
   Sunni, 43, 79

tennis *versus,* 53
   and West, 94

Islamic Movement of Uzbekistan,
   52

isolation, 11, 56

istan, 10

Jizzakh, 80

judicial branch, 46

Kara Darya, 19

Kara Kalpak people, 21

Kara Kum Canal, 68, 90

Kara Kum (Red Desert), 21

Karakalpak Republic, 24

Karakalpakistan, 87

Karakalpaks, 40, 88

Karimov, Abduganievich, 46,
   47-48, 50, 51, 52, 53, 76, 80

Karshi (Qarshi), 86, 87, 93

Karshi Steppe, 87, 94

Kashmir, 51

Kaska Darya province, 86

Kazakhs, 40

Kazakhstan, 10, 34, 88, 90

Khanabad Air Base, 93-94

Khiva, 28, 29, 30-31, 36, 47, 52,
   68, 85-86, 89

khorenizatsia (nativization), 65

Khrushchev, Nikita, 63

Khwarazm Province, 68

Kokand, 28, 29, 30-31, 34, 36,
   47, 52, 76, 77, 89

Kokcha River, 91

kolkhoz (collective farm), 34,
   46, 58-59, 61-71, 73, 84

Kolkhozabad, 90

Konduz River, 91

Koran, 42, 51, 52, 79

Koreans, 33, 76

Kyrgyz, 40

Kyrgyz reservoir system, 91
Kyrgyzstan, 10, 15, 19, 34, 88, 90, 91
Kyzyl Kum (Red Desert), 67

landlocked, Uzbekistan as, 56
language, 27, 35, 39, 40
Latin alphabet, 35, 39, 79
legislature, 46
Lenin, Vladimir Ilyich, 30
libraries, 56
lifespan, 33
literature, 26, 34, 35, 39
livestock, 54
location, 8, 10, 14, 15, 26, 94

madrassas (Islamic schools), 42, 82
mahalla (neighborhood), 37, 47
mammals, 21
manufacturing, 56, 60, 77-78, 79, 82
Marakanda, 81, 89
Margilan, 77, 78
Mecca, 42, 51
mechanical engineering plants, 56
media, 34-35, 45, 52, 53, 76
medicine, 26, 83
melons, 19, 40
Mesopotamians, 26
Middle Ages, 27-28
middle class, 60
minerals, 10, 55-56, 60, 94
minority groups, 39-40
Mongols, 27, 29
mosques, 37, 42, 52, 77, 79, 82, 83
mountains, 10, 12, 15, 16, 78
Murgab River, 90

Namangan, 34, 79
nan (bread), 40
Naryn River, 19
national consciousness, 36-43, 46-53
natural gas, 14, 55, 56, 79, 91, 95
natural resources, 10, 14, 55-56, 60, 77, 79, 91, 94, 95
nomadic groups, 34, 40
nomenclatura (elite Uzbeks), 64-65, 66
nonindigenous people, 33
Nouvruz (first day of spring), 41
nuts, 19

Oxus River, 83

packaging, 94
Pakistan, 51, 56
Pamir, 16
Pamir Knot ("Roof of the World"), 12
Pamir Mountains, 15, 16, 19
paper industry, 20, 21
people, 33-34, 36-43
Peoples' Democratic Party of Uzbekistan, 45
Persia, 27
pesticides, 22-23
Peter the Great, 29
petroleum, 10, 14, 55, 56, 79, 95
physical environment, 10, 12, 14-25
plant life, 14
political parties, 33, 37, 39, 45, 46, 52, 60, 80
population, 32-34, 79
population growth, 32-33, 92

Index

precipitation, 12, 14-16
president, 44, 46.
   See also Karimov,
     Abduganievich
prime minister, 44
Pyandzh River, 19

Qarshi Steppe Canal, 68

rail-highway-pipeline corridor,
   56
railroads, 62, 82, 86
rainfall, 12, 14-16
Rashidov, Sharaf, 52, 80
regions, 10, 63, 74-91
religion, 10, 11, 26, 34, 37-38,
   40-43, 50-51, 53, 61, 77, 79,
   82, 83, 94
Republic of Uzbekistan, formation
   of, 31
rice, 23, 77
ruling class, 60, 64-65
rural villages, 34, 37, 57-58, 59
Russian Empire
   and Bolshevik Revolution,
     30
   and conquest of Uzbekistan,
     19, 29, 36, 52, 76-77, 78,
     82, 84, 85
   and cotton, 29, 61, 82
   Great Britain *versus,* 29, 31,
     57
   and Mongols, 27.
   See also Union of Soviet
     Socialist Republic
Russian language, 39
Russians, 33-34, 39, 40, 41
Russification, 63

salt
   and Aral Sea, 21, 23-24

   and cotton, 71
   and Turin Basin, 14
Samarkand (Samarqand), 20,
   26, 27, 29, 34, 40, 48-50, 61,
   80-82, 89
secondary salinization, 24
Seljuk Turks, 27
Shakrisabz, 86
Shem, 85
silk, 19, 78
Silk Road, 27, 29, 35, 80, 81,
   82, 85, 93
silver, 56
size, 10, 32
Skobolev, General, 77
slaves, 85
Slavs, 27
snow, 15, 16
social life, 41
South Korea, 79
sports, 53
state nationalism, 36-43, 46-53,
   83-84, 92, 94
steppes, 12, 14, 15, 16, 19, 20,
   26, 67, 89
subnationalism, 47-48
Sufiism, 50-51
sum, 60
Surkan Darya province, 86
Syr Darya, 10, 18-19, 21, 67,
   68, 80
Syr Delta, 67

Tajikistan, 10, 15, 19, 51, 88,
   90
Tajiks, 40, 42, 51, 90
Taliban regime, 51, 56, 93
Tashkent, 12, 29, 33-34, 44,
   49-50, 51, 52, 60, 74-77, 83,
   84, 89
technology, 36

Tejen River, 90
telephones, 59
television, 76
temples, 27
tennis, 53
Termez, 86, 87
terrorism, 10, 51, 93
Tethis Sea, 14
textile factories, 56
Tien Shan Mountains, 15, 16
Timur (Tamerlane), 27, 48-50, 82, 86, 87
torture, 46
tourism, 78, 85
towns, 37, 58
trade, 56, 60, 63, 73, 92, 94
transportation, 33, 55, 59, 60, 62, 75, 82, 84, 94
Trans-Siberian Line, 62
tribes, 36-37
Tulyaganova, Iroda, 53
Turin Basin, 12, 14, 15, 16, 20, 23, 29
Turkey, 27, 57
Turkistan, 26, 29, 30-31, 36, 37, 90
Turkmenistan, 10, 12, 34, 68, 88, 90
Turks, 33

Uighurstan, 51
Ukrainians, 33, 39
Ulug Beg, 83
unemployment, 51, 79
Union of Soviet Socialist Republics (USSR)
    and agriculture, 58, 59. See also and cottonization, below
    and Asian republics, 90
    and cities, 60
    and cottonization, 19, 20, 31, 46, 61-70, 77, 80, 87-88
    dissolution of, 8, 31, 33, 41-42, 57, 79
    and economy, 33, 55-56, 58, 59, 60, 77. See also and agriculture, above
    and education, 34-35, 39
    formation of, 30
    and gold, 55-56
    and government, 33-34, 45, 63
    and religion, 37-38
    and sports, 53
    and Tashkent, 74-75, 77
    and Turkistan, 36, 37
    and Uzbekistan as republic within, 30-31, 36, 37, 52, 88
United States, 8, 10, 29, 61, 93-94
uranium, 56
Urganch, 85-86
Uzbek alphabet, 39
Uzbek language, 34, 35, 40
Uzbek Language Law of 1989, 34
Uzbek Soviet Socialist Republic, formation of, 30-31, 36, 37
Uzbekistan, as Land of Uzbeks, 10, 12
Uzbekization, 34, 39-40
Uzbeks, 34, 36-39, 40-43, 46, 51, 52, 57, 62-66, 90
    as Sarts (settled people), 34, 40

Vakhsh River, 19, 90
Vasco de Gama, 27
vegetables, 19, 40, 54-55
villages, 74
Volga River, 27

Index

warlordism, 10
water consumption, 70-71, 87
water features, 10
water pollution, 22-23, 71, 87-88,
   90-91
water supply, 14-16, 17-25, 32, 33,
   36, 61, 62, 63, 64, 67-71, 73, 75,
   80, 84, 87-88, 90-91, 92

winds, 14, 15
World Tennis Association, 53
World War II, 33, 62, 77, 82

youth, in population, 32, 79

Zeravshan Delta, 84
Zeravshan River, 61, 80, 82

About the Author

TOM MCCRAY is a Geography Instructor at Columbia College in Columbia, Missouri. His main interests are cultural and economic and physical geography; he lectures on Southwest Asia and nations and regions of the former Soviet Union. His research has involved circumnavigations of South America, sailing on Siberia's Lake Baikal, farming and railroading in California's San Joaquin Valley, and studying post-Soviet reforms among the Central Asian states.

CHARLES F. ("FRITZ") GRITZNER is Distinguished Professor of Geography at South Dakota University in Brookings. He is now in his fifth decade of college teaching and research. During his career, he has taught more than 60 different courses, spanning the fields of physical, cultural, and regional geography. In addition to his teaching, he enjoys writing, working with teachers, and sharing his love for geography with students. As consulting editor for the MODERN WORLD NATIONS series, he has a wonderful opportunity to combine each of these "hobbies." Fritz has served as both President and Executive Director of the National Council for Geographic Education and has received the Council's highest honor, the George J. Miller Award for Distinguished Service.